CAMBRIDGE GED PROGRAM

NEW REVISED

CAMBRIDGE GED PROGRAM

EXERCISE BOOK FOR Social Studies

Marjorie Jacobs

CAMBRIDGE ADULT EDUCATION
A Division of Simon & Schuster
Upper Saddle River, New Jersey

NEW REVISED CAMBRIDGE GED PROGRAM

WRITERS

Beverly Ann Chin
Gloria Levine
Karen Wunderman
Stella Sands
Michael Ross
Alan Hines
Donald Gerstein

CONSULTANTS/REVIEWERS

Marjorie Jacobs
Cecily Bodnar
Diane Hardison
Dr. Margaret Tinzmann
Nora Chomitz
Bert C. Honigman
Sylvester Pues

COVER

Art Director: Josée Ungaretta
Cover Design: Marta Wolchuk, Design Five, NYC
Cover Illustration: Min Jae Hong

Printed in the United States of America

3 4 5 6 7 8 9 10 01 00 99

ISBN 0-835-94732-7

CAMBRIDGE ADULT EDUCATION
A Division of Simon & Schuster
Upper Saddle River, New Jersey

Contents

Introduction

This *Exercise Book for the Social Studies Test* can provide you with practice at answering the types of questions you will find on the second test of the GED. You can use it along with either the *New Revised Cambridge GED Program: Comprehensive Book* or the *New Revised Cambridge GED Program: Social Studies.* The book has three types of exercises. The paragraphs that follow explain how to use them, the Answers and Explanations, and the Performance Analysis Charts.

The first section of exercises is grouped according to the areas of social studies. You can use any group of items after you have studied the related chapter in a *Cambridge GED Program.* For example, after you study the chapter on history, you can work through the history items. Or, you can study all of the chapters and then use the first section of exercises for general practice. It would probably be best to complete the exercises in this book before you do the Practice Items in one of the *Cambridge GED Programs.*

The two Practice Tests are like the actual Social Studies Test of the GED: the subjects covered vary from item to item. The Half-length Practice Test has 32 items—half as many as the GED's Social Studies Test. The Full-length Practice test has 64 items which you should complete in 85 minutes. You should take the Practice Tests after you have completed the exercises in the first section of this book. You might want to take these Practice Tests after you have completed the Practice Section in either *Cambridge GED Program.*

The Simulated Test is as much like the GED as possible. It has the same number of items and is as challenging as the real test. It can help you determine how ready you are for the Social Studies Test of the GED. You can take it before or after you take the Simulated Test in either *Cambridge GED Program.* Take the Simulated Test under GED-like conditions: work without interruption, do not talk to anyone or consult other materials, and time yourself.

Answers and Explanations are at the back of this book. Read through the explanations of the correct answers to reinforce your knowledge of social studies and understanding of the test-taking process.

Completing the **Performance Analysis Charts** can help you determine which skills and areas are your strongest. The charts will also direct you to parts of the *Cambridge GED Programs* you may wish to review.

History Items

Directions: Choose the one best answer for each question.

Items 1 to 3 refer to the following information.

When the American colonies were first settled, immigrants arrived from England, Northern Ireland, and Germany. Many came in the hopes of escaping poverty and/or religious oppression. During the eighteenth century and the first half of the nineteenth, immigrants continued to come in great numbers from Ireland and Germany. They came at a time of westward expansion and often participated in it. Many of these immigrants, for example, settled in the Midwest to farm the plains.

Toward the end of the nineteenth century there was a second wave of immigrants. Most of these new immigrants came from southern and eastern Europe. Italians, Serbs, and Greeks sought relief from the desperate economic conditions of their homelands. Jews from Russia and Poland fled religious persecution as well. Because they came at a time of industrial expansion, many of these "second-wave" immigrants settled in cities and worked in difficult and low-paying factory jobs.

Many other groups came, too. Japanese came to California as farm workers. Chinese came in the decades after the Civil War, often to work on the construction of the railroads.

1. Which of the following was a similarity between first-wave and second-wave immigrants?

(1) their countries of origin
(2) their reasons for coming
(3) their religion
(4) the areas of the United States in which they settled
(5) the occupations they took up in the United States

2. Which of the following groups would most likely have been found working long hours in early-twentieth-century sweatshops and factories?

(1) the Russians
(2) the Irish
(3) the Germans
(4) the Chinese
(5) the Japanese

3. It is often said that immigrants helped build America. Based on the passage, what is one reason for this statement?

(1) Immigrants came to escape poverty and religious oppression.
(2) People came to America from many different places.
(3) Immigrants played a role in both westward expansion and industrialization.
(4) Immigrants to America were generally well-educated and highly skilled.
(5) Immigrants often suffered great hardship when they first came to America.

Items 4 and 5 are based on the following map.

ELECTION OF 1860

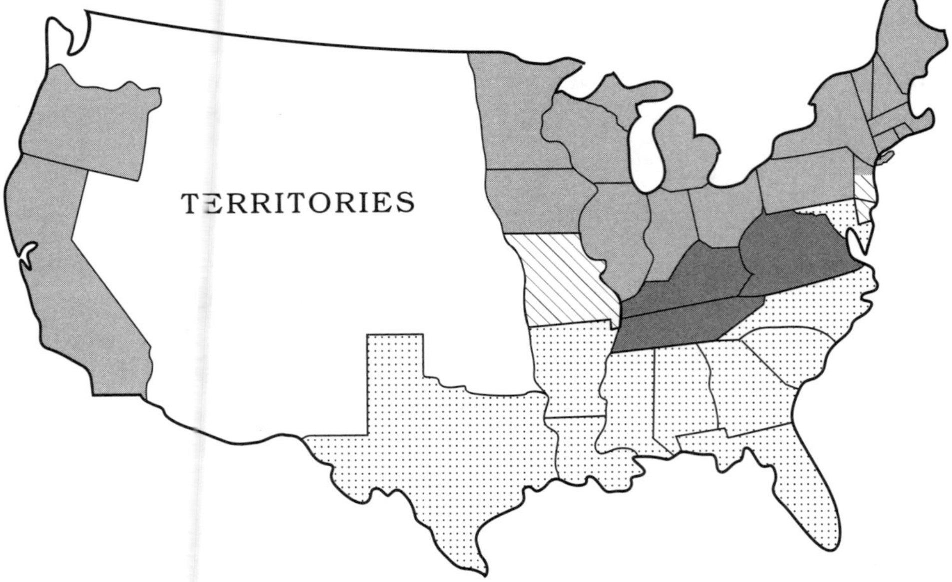

	Electoral votes	Popular votes
Lincoln (Rep.)	180	1,866,000
Douglas (No. Dem.)	12	1,375,000
Breckinridge (So. Dem.)	72	848,000
Bell (Const. Union)	39	591,000

4. Which of the following statements about the election of 1860 is <u>not</u> true?

(1) Because of their size, the territories were able to determine the outcome of the election.
(2) Lincoln won even though he didn't have a majority of the total popular vote.
(3) Douglas was able to place second in popular votes but not in electoral votes.
(4) The Democratic party was split into Northern and Southern factions.
(5) Each candidate captured at least one state.

5. Which of the following statements about U.S. politics and elections does the map suggest?

(1) The United States has a strict two-party system, and third parties are not allowed.
(2) A candidate can win an election without winning a majority of the electoral votes.
(3) The winner is chosen on the basis of the popular vote rather than the electoral vote.
(4) It is difficult for an incumbent to win reelection.
(5) States within a geographical area sometimes tend to favor the same candidate.

6. Writs of Assistance were general search warrants which authorized British colonial officials to search any place they chose and to seize any smuggled goods. Which of the following slogans most likely expresses colonists' response to these unrestricted searches?

(1) No taxation without representation.
(2) One's home is one's castle.
(3) Give me liberty or give me death.
(4) Common sense forbids a continent to be ruled by an island.
(5) All men are created equal.

Items 7 and 8 refer to the following information.

In the 1750s there were two self-governing colonies, three proprietary colonies, and eight royal colonies. Each colony had its own legislature. In the self-governing colonies, governors and legislators were elected by eligible voters. Proprietary colonies were owned by individuals or families. In these colonies, the proprietor chose the governor and eligible voters elected members of the legislature. Royal colonies were directly controlled by the British monarch. In royal colonies, eligible voters couldn't elect all legislators. They could elect only members of the lower house of the legislature.

7. There is evidence in the passage to support which one of the following statements?

(1) Colonial governors were always appointed.
(2) Most colonial legislatures had two houses.
(3) Most colonies were self-governing.
(4) Colonists elected members to the English Parliament.
(5) Colonial legislatures were first created in the 1750s.

8. Which of the following statements is a conclusion supported by the passage?

(1) Americans had no political experience until after the Revolution.
(2) Some colonies enjoyed more democracy than others.
(3) Colonial governors had unlimited powers.
(4) All colonists were eligible to vote.
(5) Colonial legislatures imposed heavy taxes on the colonists.

Item 9 refers to the following map.

PACIFIC NORTH AMERICA, 1846

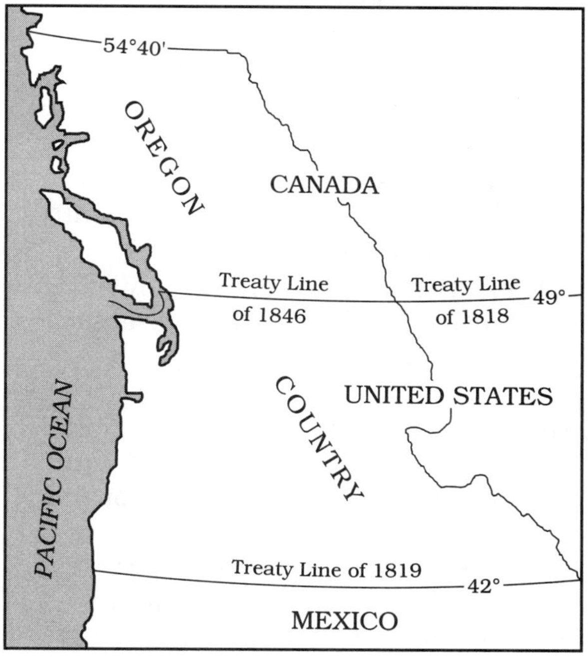

9. Which of the following statements is best supported by the map?

(1) By 1818 the present-day northern border of the United States was fully established.
(2) By 1846 the present-day northern border of the United States was fully established.
(3) By 1846 the present-day southern border of the United States was fully established.
(4) The Treaty of 1846 was signed with Mexico.
(5) In 1846 the United States acquired all of the vast territory known as Oregon Country.

10. The Federalists were an important party in the early years of this nation. The party was made up mainly of wealthy people, including bankers and manufacturers. Federalists wanted the national government to be much stronger than the state governments. They distrusted the common people and wanted democracy, including voting rights, to be limited.

To which of the following would the Federalists most likely have objected?

(1) a restriction saying that only property owners could vote
(2) a high tariff on imported goods to protect American manufacturers
(3) a law that strengthened the country's banking system
(4) measures that shifted power from the national government to state and local governments
(5) election of U.S. senators by state legislators, rather than directly by the voters

11. Under the Articles of Confederation, Congress did not have the power to control interstate commerce. Nor did it have the power to control commerce with foreign countries. Each state made up its own regulations and tariffs (taxes) for interstate and foreign commerce.

Which of the following statements concerning trade under the Articles of Confederation is <u>least</u> likely correct?

(1) Tariffs and taxes were the same from state to state.
(2) Trade between states was marked by disputes and disagreements.
(3) States taxed each other's goods.
(4) Britain refused trade agreements with the United States because Congress had no power to enforce them.
(5) A multitude of different regulations led to a confused situation.

Items 12 and 13 refer to the following quote.

Depend upon it, Sir, it is dangerous to open so fruitful a source of controversy and altercation as would be opened by attempting to alter the qualifications of voters; there will be no end of it. New claims will arise; women will demand a vote, lads from twelve to twenty-one will think their rights are not enough attended to, and every man who has not a farthing will demand an equal voice with any other in all acts of state. It tends to confound and destroy all distinctions, and prostrate all ranks to the common level.

—John Adams

12. Which of the following situations evidently existed at the time of the quote?

(1) The United States was involved in great turmoil and conflict.
(2) The vote had recently been extended to all adult citizens.
(3) Women were unable to vote.
(4) Compulsory education was being introduced into the schools.
(5) The Industrial Revolution was reducing social class differences.

13. John Adams evidently believed that

(1) slavery was undemocratic and should be abolished
(2) all citizens should be given an equal voice in government
(3) great changes were needed in the American political system
(4) some people were better qualified to participate in the political system than others
(5) the American political system wasn't sufficiently democratic

Item 14 is based on the following cartoon.

There's a long, long trail a-winding—

14. Which of the following statements best expresses the message of the cartoon?

(1) Civil rights bills have been passed because many Americans worked hard to ensure their passage.
(2) Civil rights legislation has had a greater effect on the South than on the North.
(3) Civil rights legislation has brought full civil rights to all Americans.
(4) The greatest impact of civil rights legislation has come in the area of voting rights.
(5) Civil rights legislation is just a necessary first step on the way to full civil rights for all Americans.

Items 15 and 16 are based on the following information.

About 80 percent of white families in the South held no slaves. They worked their land themselves. Nevertheless, these nonslaveholders strongly supported slavery. Slavery gave them someone to look down on and allowed them to identify themselves with the wealthy slave-holding whites. The slave owners themselves, of course, were even less willing to reject slavery. They saw the prosperity of their cotton plantations as depending on slave labor. When abolitionists attacked slavery, they defended it. They even argued that slavery was sanctioned by the Bible.

15. Which of the following best summarizes the purpose of the passage?

(1) to trace the origins of slavery in the South
(2) to describe abolitionist arguments against slavery
(3) to describe the growth of the abolitionist movement in the North
(4) to show how slavery helped the South's economy
(5) to give reasons why slavery persisted in the South

16. Based on the information, which of the following statements accurately expresses a sociological and psychological explanation for slavery?

(1) Slavery was sanctioned by the Bible.
(2) The existence of slavery helped Southern whites who weren't wealthy feel better about their own position in society.
(3) The South's economy was based on cotton, and slaves worked the cotton plantations.
(4) White Southerners were afraid of slave uprisings like Nat Turner's rebellion.
(5) Many Southern families had no slaves.

Item 17 is based on the following cartoon.

It's going to be just turned around

17. In the 1920s, spurred by growing isolationist sentiment, fear of foreign radicals, and at least to some extent by prejudice, Congress passed several immigration laws. A quota system was thereby established, restricting immigration, especially immigration from certain religions. These immigration laws were hotly debated.

What position was the cartoonist taking with regard to one such law?

(1) The proposed law was going to produce undesirable confusion in immigration procedures at Ellis Island and other entry points.
(2) The proposed law would in fact have very little effect, and, as a result, "undesirables" would still enter this country.
(3) The proposed law was irrational and discriminatory.
(4) The law would result in better, more rational procedures without having any undesirable consequences.
(5) The new law would completely turn things around, encouraging native-born Americans to emigrate from the United States.

18. In 1793, Eli Whitney invented the cotton gin. Thanks to this machine, the previously time-consuming task of separating cotton seed from cotton fiber became simple and inexpensive. Which of the following was the most likely effect of this invention on the South?

(1) The plantation system was destroyed.
(2) The amount of land under cultivation decreased.
(3) The South became a major exporter of machinery and other manufactured goods.
(4) The South was able to produce much more cotton than before.
(5) Many farmers switched from cotton cultivation to tobacco cultivation.

Items 19 to 21 are based on the following information.

In 1890 only about one American in three lived in a city, but by 1910 nearly half the U.S. population was urban. Cities lacked the intimacy, self-sufficiency, spaciousness, and leisurely pace of small-town, rural America. Thousands of people were concentrated in relatively small areas. They typically rose early in the morning to race to work and rushed home after dark to eat and sleep, hardly having the time to exchange more than a few words with their neighbors.

Because space in cities was limited, buildings grew taller and taller. Sunlight and fresh air gave way to pollution from factory smokestacks. Parks were among the few open spaces remaining for city dwellers to stretch their legs and enjoy their leisure.

Among households in rural America there were small differences in economic status. However, in urban areas classes of very rich and very poor people grew. In one part of a city, the poor crowded into dingy tenements that had limited sanitation facilities. They worked long hours for low wages. When too old or sick to work, they were often left to fend for themselves or were shunted off to "poor houses." At the same time the numbers of the wealthy were increasing. They maintained splendid houses and lived out their lives in financial security.

19. Which of the following statements best summarizes the passage?

(1) Urbanization occurred in a relatively short time.
(2) Urbanization was caused largely by industrialization.
(3) Urban life was more hurried than rural life.
(4) Urbanization changed the way of life of many Americans.
(5) Working conditions and wages in cities were often not good.

20. Which of the following statements seems best to characterize the view of urbanization that is expressed in the information?

(1) The urbanization of America was unnecessary.
(2) The urbanization of America brought many problems.
(3) The urbanization of America brought immediate benefits to large numbers of citizens.
(4) Urbanization made the nation prosperous.
(5) Urbanization had little impact on American society.

21. Based on the information, what was the immediate effect of urbanization on social class structure?

(1) The gap between the rich and the poor decreased.
(2) The middle class grew in size and importance.
(3) The lower class grew in size, while the upper class disappeared.
(4) Both the upper class and the lower class increased in size.
(5) The social class structure that characterized rural America was brought to the cities.

Items 22 and 23 refer to the following graph.

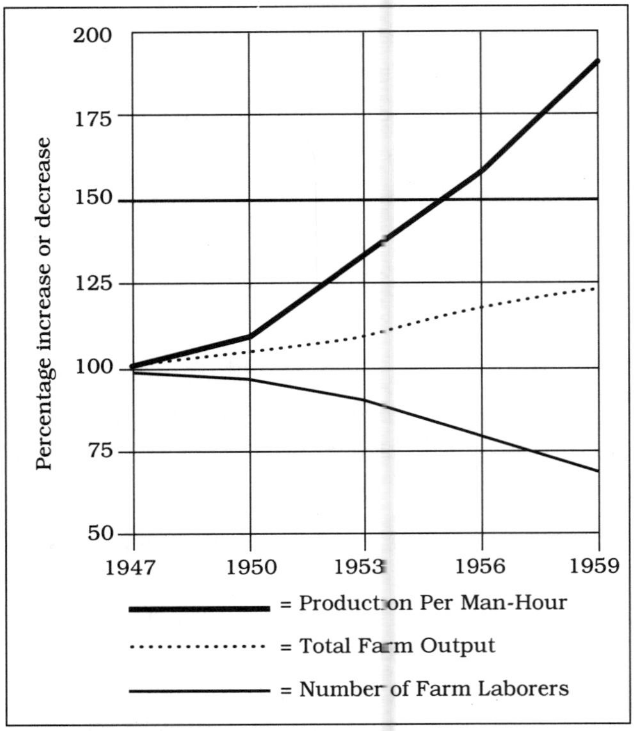

TRENDS IN AGRICULTURE, 1947-1959

---

22. The 1950s was a time of great technological advances. One area that really felt the impact of these advances was agriculture. According to the graph, farm laborers were affected by technology because it

(1) created more jobs for farm laborers
(2) reduced the need for farm laborers
(3) made farm laborers work harder to produce the same amount of goods
(4) allowed many farmers to become wealthy
(5) led to the breakup of large farms

23. The changes in agriculture shown in the graph were probably felt in the supermarket in which of the following ways?

(1) Prices fell because farmers produced more and produced more efficiently.
(2) Prices fell because of the inferior quality of agricultural goods produced with the new technology.
(3) Prices climbed sharply because a larger portion of total farm output was being exported to other countries.
(4) There was a shortage of farm products as a result of a shortage of farm laborers.
(5) There was a shortage of farm products because the nation's population increased but its total farm output didn't.

Item 24 refers to the following cartoon.

"A hand is better than a hand-out, right?"

24. According to the cartoon, which of the following types of programs would have been given lowest priority in President Johnson's War on Poverty?

(1) job training programs for unemployed youths
(2) education programs for underprivileged children
(3) programs to help inner-city communities develop new businesses
(4) programs giving funds to low-income families
(5) programs training volunteers to assist the poor

25. Before Andrew Jackson, most presidents believed that a wealthy, well-educated "elite" should govern in the interest of the people. Andrew Jackson, in contrast, believed the people themselves should have a large say in governmental affairs.

All of the following developments during Jackson's presidency are directly related to Jackson's desire to put into effect his idea of democracy except

(1) property qualifications for voting were removed
(2) many officials were now elected by voters instead of being appointed by state legislatures
(3) terms of office were shortened to give people more control over elected officials
(4) presidential electors were to be chosen directly by the voters
(5) voters increasingly focused on regional issues and split along regional lines

Items 26 and 27 are based on the following information.

Reformers of the early nineteenth century attacked a wide range of social problems. At the time, however, not much was known about the cause of such problems. Reform leaders naively believed the problems were simply the result of the weakness of individuals. If individuals could be "improved," they thought, the problems could be solved. They didn't realize that sometimes it's the society and its laws that must be changed.

26. Based on the information, the importance of early-nineteenth-century reformers was most likely that they

(1) drew people's attention to social problems
(2) discovered the main causes of social problems
(3) permanently solved a wide range of social problems
(4) introduced into America reforms begun overseas
(5) developed a model for tackling social problems that is used even today

27. Which of the following approaches to the problems of labor was most likely to have been taken by early-nineteenth-century reformers?

(1) demanding laws to improve factory safety
(2) initiating campaigns to get workers to stop drinking
(3) organizing worker movements for a shorter work week
(4) joining protests for higher wages
(5) fighting for the end of child labor in factories

Items 28 to 30 are based on the following information.

The French and Indian War (1754-1763) was a great triumph for Britain. The British were, however, bothered by the huge cost of war. They felt the North American colonists had gained much from the war, but had not helped meet the expense.

Shortly after the war Britain passed a series of measures. The Quartering Act said that from now on colonists would supply British troops with food and housing. Several of the measures passed were taxes on the colonies—both import duties and internal taxes. The Sugar Act taxed sugar imported into the colonies. The Stamp Act required colonists to buy special stamps to put on all printed materials they sold or circulated. The Townshend Acts placed a tariff on imports of glass, paper, paint, and tea. The colonists opposed these measures, so Britain restated its right to tax the colonists by passing the Declaratory Act. The Revolutionary War began in little more than a decade.

28. Based on the information, the measures passed by Britain are best seen as an attempt to

(1) encourage more British citizens to emigrate to the colonies
(2) keep the colonists happy
(3) avoid future expenses by ignoring colonists' defense needs
(4) force the colonists to help pay for their defense
(5) substitute internal taxes for import duties

29. Which of the acts was an internal tax act?

(1) Quartering Act
(2) Sugar Act
(3) Stamp Act
(4) Townshend Acts
(5) Declaratory Act

30. Which of the following best expresses the historical importance of the measures discussed?

(1) Britain was able to triumph over France in the French and Indian War.
(2) Relations between Britain and its North American colonies temporarily improved.
(3) Taxes imposed on people living in Britain dropped significantly.
(4) Colonial dissatisfaction helped to fuel a movement for independence.
(5) Other colonial powers followed the British example and began taxing their own colonies.

Items 31 to 34 refer to the following information.

A cornerstone of the women's liberation movement was Betty Friedan's *The Feminine Mystique*, published in 1963. Friedan contrasted the exaggerated respect paid to women with the superior attitude this respect often hides. She argued that women were dissatisfied with the limited role society forced them to play. Women wanted to have more choices. They wanted to be able to pursue careers. Furthermore, although the truly restrictive laws had already been changed, women still didn't have full equality. In 1966 Friedan and others formed the National Organization for Women to help change society's attitudes and to remove, by peaceful methods, legal barriers to the full equality of women.

31. Which of the following was Friedan arguing in *The Feminine Mystique*?

(1) Men should trade places with women.
(2) Women want to be placed on a pedestal and worshipped by men.
(3) Women are in fact superior to men.
(4) Self-fulfillment is an important goal of modern women.
(5) A woman's worst enemy is other women.

32. Which of the following statements best summarizes the content of the passage?

(1) *The Feminine Mystique* taught women how to be more attractive looking and alluring.
(2) The women's liberation movement arose from a sense of dissatisfaction and a demand for equality.
(3) The National Organization for Women was founded in 1966.
(4) The National Organization for Women sought to free women from the bondage of marriage.
(5) There are no longer any legal barriers to women's equality.

33. Which of the following conditions most likely explains why Friedan wrote *The Feminine Mystique*?

(1) State laws prevented women from owning property in their own name.
(2) The Constitution barred women from holding public office.
(3) Married women were legally in the custody of their husbands and had great difficulties in obtaining divorces.
(4) Society restricted most women to household and family responsibilities.
(5) In many firms most top executive positions went to women.

34. In which of the following activities would the National Organization for Women most likely be involved?

(1) seeking passage of a constitutional amendment establishing equal rights for women

(2) fighting to obtain voting rights for women

(3) petitioning for laws that would keep drunk drivers off the road

(4) establishing committees to address the issue of educational standards in America

(5) encouraging housewives to publish books about their experiences

Item 35 refers to the following cartoon.

Hesse, *St. Louis Globe-Democrat*

Rocky soil

35. To which of the following U.S. policies might this cartoon be relevant?

(1) the Monroe Doctrine, closing the Western Hemisphere to European influence

(2) the Roosevelt Corollary, authorizing U.S. intervention in Latin America to collect foreign debts

(3) dollar diplomacy, offering U.S. businessmen full government diplomatic and military support for their Latin American investments

(4) the Rio Inter-American Defense Treaty, providing for mutual defense by the United States and Latin American countries against outside aggression

(5) the Alliance for Progress, making extensive aid and trade programs available to Latin American countries that undertook social and economic reforms

Answers are on pages 126-129.

Geography Items

Directions: Choose the one best answer for each question.

Item 1 is based on the following paragraph.

Conservation of natural resources refers to attempts to preserve the materials of nature that we use. The goal is to preserve enough supplies of these resources to meet present and future needs.

1. Which of the following is <u>not</u> an example of conservation?

(1) turning down the heat to save energy
(2) planting trees to replace trees that have been cut down
(3) burning oil instead of coal
(4) protecting soil from erosion
(5) recycling newspapers and aluminum cans

Items 2 and 3 refer to the following information.

Natural hazards are possible or probable events in the natural physical environment that can be harmful to humans. Yet, people settle and remain in areas with known natural hazards. They may be drawn to a hazardous region by employment opportunities. Once there, people tend to focus on the low odds of anything happening. They support this idea with their experience, whatever that has been: If nothing has happened since they have lived in the area, they say this shows that the hazard has been exaggerated. And if, on the contrary, they have experienced an earthquake, flood, or whatever hazardous event the area is prone to, they say it has already happened and therefore will not happen again for years.

2. Which of the following is not an example of an environment with a natural hazard?

(1) an area along a river that tends to flood
(2) an area in an earthquake zone
(3) an area that contains a toxic waste dump
(4) a coastal area prone to violent storms
(5) an area near an active volcano

3. According to the passage, people are not afraid to stay in areas that have known natural hazards because

(1) they are unaware of the hazards
(2) their experience with past hazardous events has taught them how to deal with such events
(3) they manage to convince themselves that nothing will happen to them
(4) they trust scientists who say that the odds of anything happening are low
(5) they would not be able to find work or housing anywhere else

Item 4 is based on the following graphs.

AIR POLLUTION EMISSIONS IN THE UNITED STATES
(in percentages by weight)

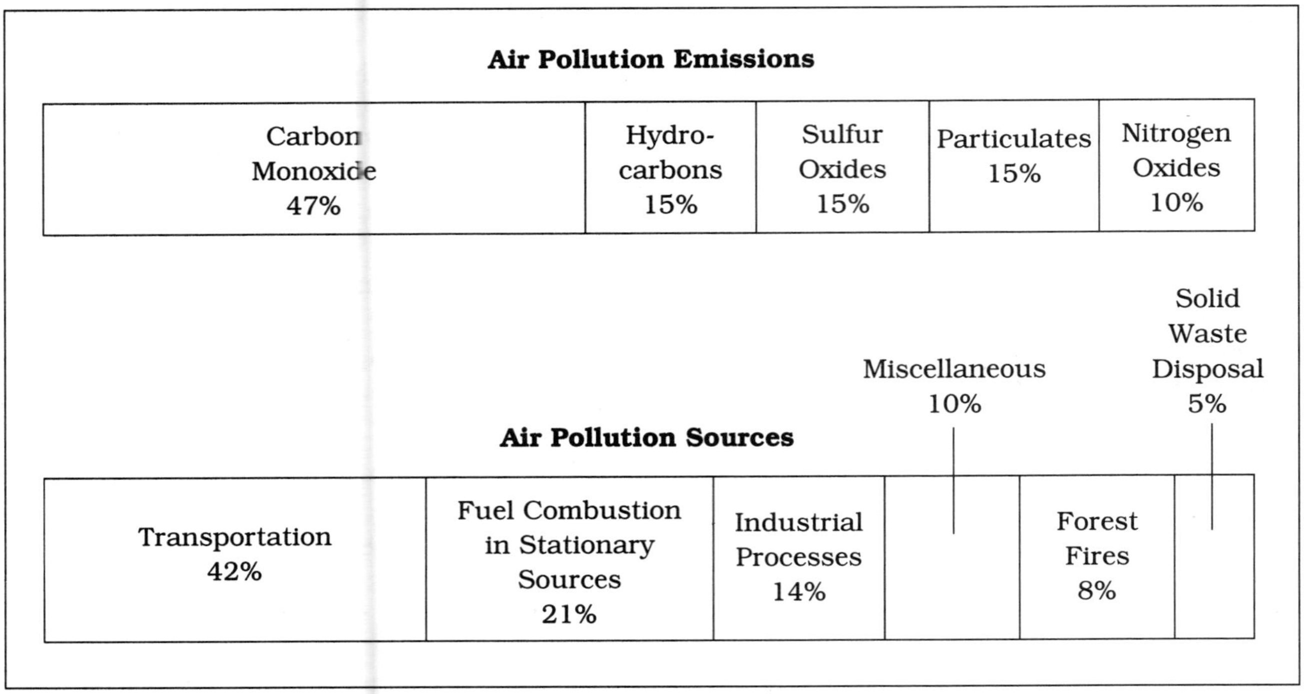

Source: National Air Pollution Control Administration

4. Which conclusion can you draw from the information in one or both of the graphs?

(1) Air pollution is the most serious form of pollution.
(2) Solid waste disposal is the main source of carbon monoxide.
(3) Hydrocarbons are the main pollutants.
(4) Much of the air pollution problem is caused by miscellaneous sources.
(5) Most U.S. air pollution results from heating buildings and driving vehicles.

5. Any geographical area can be said to have a certain carrying capacity. That is, any area's agricultural and other resources will support only up to a certain amount of people. The approximate number of people an area can support with these resources is its carrying capacity.

Which of the following statements is not consistent with the information above?

(1) Different areas have different carrying capacities.
(2) The carrying capacity of an area is not entirely fixed by nature but can be altered somewhat by humans.
(3) Soil and climate are important factors in determining an area's carrying capacity.
(4) An area with extensive farming likely has a high carrying capacity.
(5) The earth as a whole can support an unlimited number of people.

Items 6 to 8 are based on the following table.

Country	Total Area (sq. miles)	Farmland (sq. miles)	Percentage of Land Used as Farmland	Population
Australia	2,966,200	1,852,500	63	15,912,000
Brazil	3,286,500	1,408,100	43	138,403,000
Canada	3,849,675	254,300	7	25,640,000
China	3,696,100	399,100	11	1,053,703,000
India	1,183,427	630,400	50	777,230,000
Commwealth of Independent States (formerly Soviet Union)	8,649,500	2,337,600	27	280,038,000
United States	3,623,461	1,586,900	43	241,489,000
Zaire	905,365	22,800	3	31,079,000

6. Of the countries listed in the table, which one has the least farmland relative to its overall size?

(1) Australia
(2) Brazil
(3) Commonwealth of Independent States
(4) United States
(5) Zaire

7. The statistics on which country most effectively demonstrate that larger countries don't always have the largest proportions of farmland?

(1) Brazil
(2) Canada
(3) India
(4) Commonwealth of Independent States
(5) United States

8. Based on the table, which country is least likely to be a major importer of food?

(1) Australia
(2) Canada
(3) China
(4) United States
(5) Zaire

9. Gradational processes are natural phenomena that have the effect of gradually reducing the amount of land there is. Which of the following is an example of a gradational process and its effects?

(1) Mountains are slowly formed as the earth is thrust upward when pressure causes layers of rock to buckle.
(2) A coastline gradually moves inland because over time the sea has carried rock and soil particles away.
(3) Cities expand rapidly as large numbers of people migrate to an area.
(4) The earth's climate changes slowly over time as its orbit around the sun changes.
(5) Farmland eventually loses its fertility as a result of overuse.

Items 10 and 11 are based on the following map.

ASIA: FOOD SUPPLY BY COUNTRY

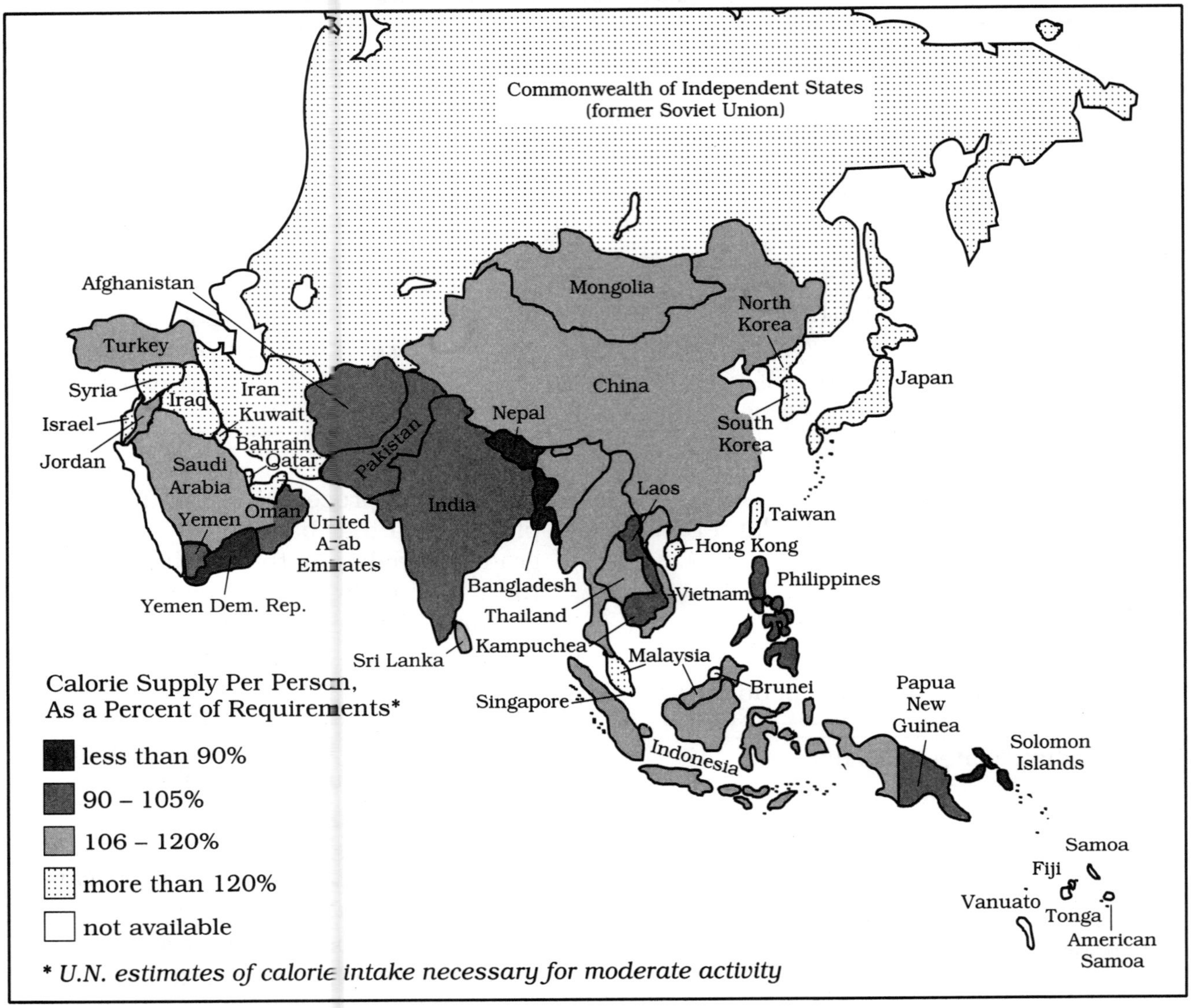

Source: World Population Data Sheet, Population Reference Bureau, 1993

10. This map of Asia can be used to find out

(1) which countries have the most factories

(2) which countries have the largest populations

(3) what political system each country has

(4) how many hungry people there are in each country

(5) how adequate each country's food supply is

11. Suppose you wanted to argue that lack of land doesn't always mean a limited food supply. Which of the following countries could you use to support that argument?

(1) Bangladesh

(2) China

(3) Japan

(4) Laos

(5) Commonwealth of Independent States

Items 12 to 14 are based on the following charts.

Climates may be classified by amount of rainfall, as well as by temperature. A common classification of climate by amount of rainfall is as follows:

tropical rainy	—	more than 80" of rain a year
humid	—	about 20-60" of rain a year
semiarid	—	10-15" of rain a year
arid	—	5-9" of rain a year
desert	—	less than 4" of rain a year

The following table gives normal annual rainfall for selected areas in the United States.

Place	Normal Annual Rainfall
Furnace Creek, California	1.66
Phoenix, Arizona	7.05
Albuquerque, New Mexico	7.77
Winnemucca, Nevada	8.47
Denver, Colorado	15.51
Burlington, Vermont	32.54
Chicago, Illinois	34.44
Cleveland, Ohio	34.99
Portland, Oregon	37.61
Seattle, Washington	38.79
Key West, Florida	39.99
Hartford, Connecticut	43.37
Montgomery, Alabama	49.86
Mount Waialeale, Hawaii	460.00

12. Which two places that have a humid climate have higher average rainfall amounts than Key West, Florida?

(1) Hartford and Seattle
(2) Hartford and Montgomery
(3) Portland and Seattle
(4) Montgomery and Mount Waialeale
(5) Burlington and Seattle

13. Since the Southwest receives the least amount of rainfall per year, you can conclude that its climate is

(1) very hot
(2) tropical
(3) extremely cold
(4) arid
(5) desert

14. Which of the following statements about the climate of the United States is best supported by the information given?

(1) Much of the United States has very definite seasons, with hot summers and cold winters.
(2) Much of the United States has a semi-arid climate.
(3) Much of the United States has a humid climate.
(4) The United States contains large areas that belong to each of the five different climate types based on amount of rainfall.
(5) The southern half of the United States has basically the same rainfall levels throughout.

Items 15 and 16 refer to the following paragraph.

Continentality refers to the effect that large land masses have on temperature and precipitation. The Commonwealth of Independent States (formerly Soviet Union) provides a good example. Like all large land masses, it loses heat rapidly. And since much of the land is far from the sea, the air usually contains little moisture.

15. Based on the information, the Commonwealth of Independent States likely has

(1) a hot, desert-like climate
(2) a humid, tropical climate
(3) mild weather all year long
(4) long, severe winters
(5) long periods of heavy rainfall

16. Great Britain is about the same distance from the equator as the Commonwealth of Independent States but is not characterized by continentality. Compared to the climate of the Commonwealth of Independent States, Britain's climate should be

(1) warmer and rainier
(2) warmer and drier
(3) colder and drier
(4) colder and snowier
(5) more extreme in both summer and winter

Item 17 refers to the following diagram.

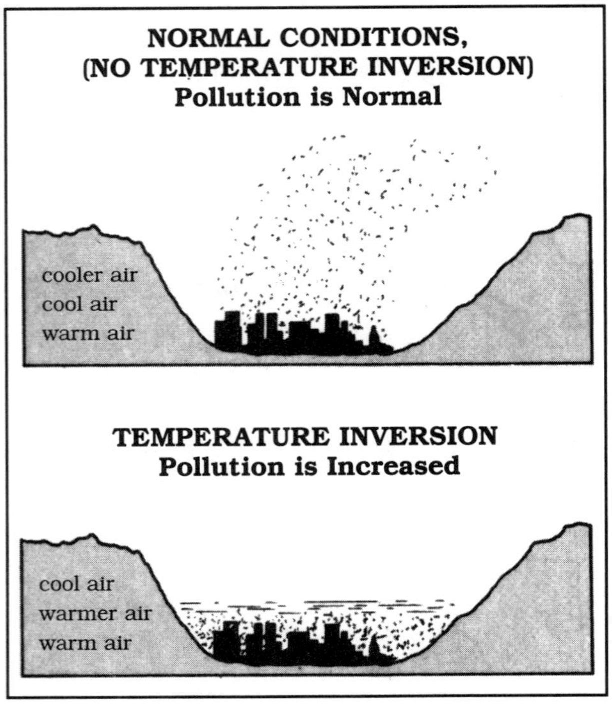

17. The figures show how air pollution can be increased during temperature inversion. Pollution increases during an inversion (as contrasted with normal conditions) because

(1) more pollution from factories is released into the air
(2) air temperatures at different altitudes vary
(3) the layer of warm air at the very lowest altitude traps pollution
(4) the layer of warmer air above the warm surface air traps pollution
(5) mountains prevent air currents from removing pollution

Items 18 and 19 refer to the following paragraphs.

Flat maps are much easier to store and use than globes. But, since the earth is round, only a globe can accurately represent area, shape, distance, and direction at the same time. Any flat map will distort at least one of these features.

Flat maps are made by projecting the globe, or part of it, onto a flat surface. Geographers may use any of several different projections in making a map. The purpose of the map will determine what kind of distortions are acceptable.

18. Which of the following is the most appropriate title for the passage?

(1) The History of Maps
(2) Who Makes Maps?
(3) Flat Maps Misrepresent Round Earth
(4) The Many Uses of Road Maps
(5) What's on a Map?

19. Which of the following statements about distortions on maps is supported by information in the passage?

(1) Shape is a feature that can never be accurately represented on a map.
(2) Some projections make it possible to eliminate distortions on maps altogether.
(3) Different projections produce different kinds of distortions.
(4) All maps have the same types and amount of distortion.
(5) Because of their distortions, maps have no advantages over globes.

Item 20 is based on the following map.

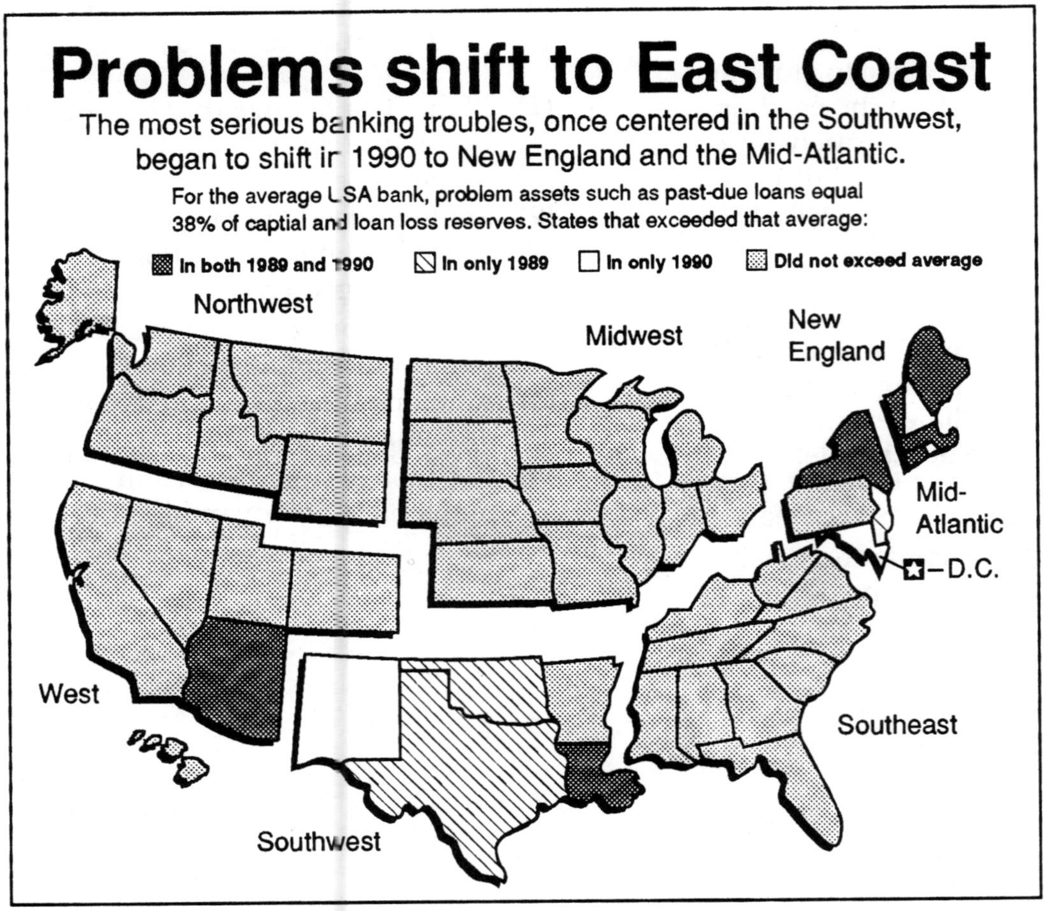

From USA Today, 5/28/91. Copyright © 1991, USA Today. Reprinted with permission.

20. If you wanted to move your family to an area of the U.S. that did not experience banking problems from 1989-1990, has a warm climate year round, and is located near your relatives in the Caribbean, where would you go?

(1) the Southeast
(2) the Southwest
(3) the West
(4) the Midwest
(5) the Mid-Atlantic

Answers are on pages 129–130.

Economics Items

Directions: Choose the one best answer for each question.

Items 1 and 2 are based on the following information.

Today only about 20 percent of all American workers belong to labor unions. Yet the power of unions is greater than this figure would seem to indicate. One reason for this is that unions are concentrated in the major manufacturing areas of our economy. This concentration gives unions strength. In recent years, however, the manufacturing sector has suffered economic setbacks. This has, in turn, hurt the unions.

1. Which of the following statements is best supported by the passage?

(1) Unions' concentration is the source of their strength and of their weakness.
(2) Labor unions are gradually dying out.
(3) Strikes have become more common in recent years.
(4) Unions have a powerful lobby in Congress.
(5) The different unions have a hard time agreeing with one another on issues.

2. Forty years ago, 25 percent of all American workers belonged to unions. Based on the information, the likeliest reason for today's lower union membership is

(1) the passage of anti-union legislation
(2) layoffs of large numbers of manufacturing workers
(3) the increased power of the unions
(4) changes in income tax rates for workers
(5) more on-the-job training for workers

Item 3 is based on the following information.

In recent years many companies have been using "negative advertising." That is, they try to sell their products by criticizing their competitors' products. A study of different advertising approaches found that consumers had negative reactions to negative ads. Interestingly, consumers indicated they were most inclined to believe, and therefore trust, companies that mentioned negatives in connection with their <u>own</u> products.

3. According to the study, an effective advertising slogan might be:

(1) Brand X runs down quickly; <u>our</u> brand lasts.
(2) Brand X or our brand?—<u>You</u> be the judge.
(3) We offer you the ultimate in luxuries—at the lowest of prices.
(4) No trimmings—but the service is efficient and the price is right.
(5) Nine out of ten experts agree: Our product is the best!

Item 4 is based on the following graph.

EARNINGS BY BUSINESS TYPE

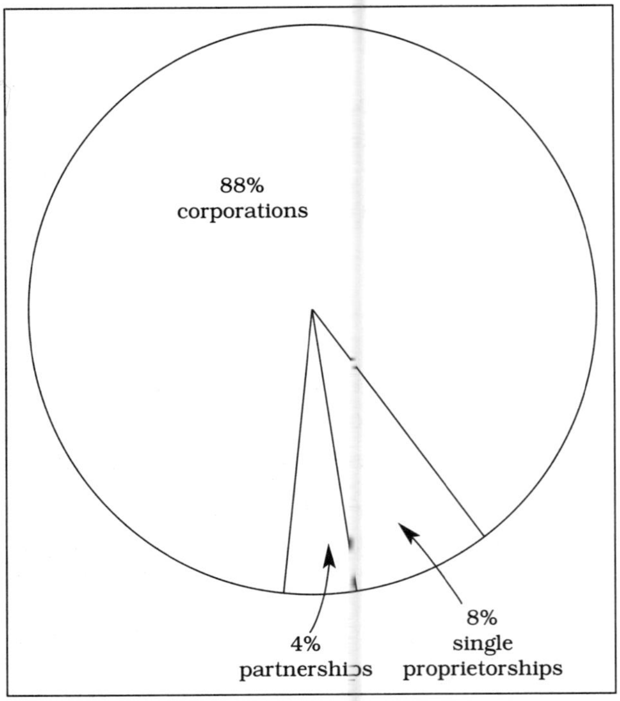

4. The graph shows how total business earnings are divided among businesses by organization type. Which of the following facts explains why earning rates per organization type are so different?

(1) Over 75 percent of the businesses in the United States are single proprietorships.
(2) Large businesses are almost always organized as corporations.
(3) In a partnership the responsibilities of business can be spread among more people than in a single proprietorship.
(4) To protect stockholders the government regulates corporations more than other types of businesses.
(5) Single proprietorships are the easiest form of business to start.

Items 5 to 8 are based on the following information.

Economists generally classify unemployment into four categories. Each of these four kinds of unemployment has a different cause.

<u>Cyclical unemployment</u> is caused by a general slowdown in the nation's economy. Businesses can't sell as many goods. So they don't produce as much, and they don't need as many employees. Workers are laid off, except industries that provide essential goods or services.

<u>Structural unemployment</u> is caused by fundamental changes in the way a particular industry operates. When an industry adopts a new technology, for example, there may be fewer of certain jobs in that industry. Some kinds of jobs may even disappear.

<u>Seasonal unemployment</u> is the temporary unemployment that occurs in industries that need lots of workers only during certain parts of the year. The ski industry, for example, needs workers mainly in winter.

<u>Frictional unemployment</u> results when an individual quits a job or is fired. It has nothing to do with the overall economy or with particular industries.

5. Which of the following individuals is frictionally unemployed?

(1) Peter just finished school and is looking for his first job.
(2) Paul worked as a waiter in a winter resort, but his restaurant closed down at the end of February.
(3) Bill quit his job because he and his boss didn't get along.
(4) Sarah's factory stopped production because consumers weren't buying enough cars.
(5) Ben, an elevator operator, hasn't worked since his building switched to an automatic elevator.

6. Individuals should be advised to retrain and look for a new kind of job if the unemployment they experience is

(1) cyclical
(2) structural
(3) frictional
(4) seasonal
(5) sometimes seasonal and sometimes frictional

7. Which of the following workers is most likely to become seasonally unemployed?

(1) a bank teller
(2) a typist
(3) a janitor
(4) a lifeguard
(5) a dental technician

8. Which of the following workers is *least* likely to become cyclically unemployed?

(1) an appliance salesperson
(2) a surgeon
(3) a worker in an automobile factory
(4) a worker in the garment industry
(5) a children's book editor

Items 9 and 10 are based on the following table.

Mothers Participating in the Labor Force
(as a percentage of all women with children in that age category)

Mothers With Children			
Year	Under 6 Years Old	6 to 17 Years Old	Under 18 Years Old
1950	13.6	32.8	21.6
1955	18.2	38.4	27.0
1965	25.3	45.7	35.0
1975	38.9	54.8	47.4
1980	46.6	64.4	56.6
1986	54.4	70.4	62.8

Source: Bureau of Labor Statistics

9. The trend this table shows is an increase in

(1) the number of college-educated women
(2) the national birthrate
(3) the number of women in the workforce
(4) the percentage of women who are mothers
(5) the percentage of mothers who work

10. From the information in this table, you could conclude that there has also been an increase in

(1) the number of children who receive some form of child care
(2) the size of the average American family
(3) the unemployment rate
(4) the size of an average family's financial indebtedness
(5) the number of single mothers who must support themselves

Items 11 to 13 are based on the following passage.

In the past, a workman not trained in the business of pinmaking could scarcely make one pin in a day. He certainly could not make twenty.

But the way in which this business is now carried on, not only is the entire manufacture one trade, but it is divided into a number of branches. One man draws out the wire, another straightens it, a third cuts it, a fourth points it, a fifth grinds it at the top for receiving the head; to make the head requires two or three distinct operations. To put it on is another. To whiten the pins is still another. . . . In this manner, the important business of making a pin is divided into about eighteen separate operations, which in some factories are all performed by different hands.

Even if these workers were all, individually, very poor workers, they could, when they exerted themselves, make upwards of forty-eight thousand pins in a day. If each had worked individually, without having been trained in this particular industry, none could have made more than twenty.

Adapted from: Adam Smith, *The Wealth of Nations* (1776)

11. What major change in the production process is described in the passage?

(1) Production was no longer carried on in the home.
(2) Production was broken down into small, easily accomplished steps.
(3) Production came to rely heavily on machines.
(4) Production became slower and less efficient.
(5) Production, overall, was vastly simplified.

12. Compared to pinmakers of an earlier time, the latter-day pinmakers described needed

(1) more skills
(2) fewer skills
(3) similar skills
(4) new skills
(5) no skills

13. Which of the following would be the most likely result of the changes described in the passage?

(1) The new pins would be less useful than the old pins.
(2) Pinmaking would become less profitable as a business.
(3) Pins would become scarce and difficult for consumers to find.
(4) Pinmakers would be forced to charge more for their pins.
(5) Pins would become more plentiful and cheaper.

14. About 10,000 years ago, some societies gave up hunting and settled in one place to farm. Farming yielded more food than hunting in the same amount of time and with similar effort. As a result, those societies' standards of living rose.

If a modern nation wants to improve its standard of living, it must

(1) promote farming
(2) increase production
(3) reduce the number of people in farming
(4) shorten the work week
(5) encourage more people to settle in cities

Items 15 to 17 are based on the following information.

Recent years have seen a decline in the number of blue-collar, factory jobs. In 1980, 21 million Americans were employed in factory jobs. By 1986, only six years later, 2 million of these jobs had vanished. Some observers feel this decline in factory jobs is a sign that America's economy is in trouble.

Others, however, disagree. They point out that despite the decline in factory jobs, unemployment in America did not increase. On the contrary, unemployment decreased.

Unemployment did not increase because in the same six-year period, 6 million new service jobs opened up. Service jobs, as their name implies, provide services rather than products. Waitresses, salespeople, computer programmers, doctors, and lawyers all work in service jobs.

Within the area of service jobs, professional, managerial, and technical workers are especially in demand. These workers must be well trained, and they must be able to work with ideas and information. Government statistics indicate that, at least through the end of the century, the job market will be strongest for these three kinds of service jobs.

15. Which of the following statements best summarizes the passage?

(1) Jobs in sales and computer programming provide services.
(2) Government statistics predict what the job market will be like for different kinds of jobs.
(3) An increase in service jobs more than made up for a decline in the number of blue-collar jobs.
(4) Competition from manufacturers abroad caused the decline in the number of American blue-collar jobs.
(5) Changes in the job market helped some parts of the country but hurt others.

16. Based on the information, what advice could be offered to a person who will be entering the job market?

(1) Unemployment is being eliminated, so it will be easy to find a job.
(2) Rapid changes in recent years make it impossible to guess what kinds of jobs will be available.
(3) Education and training will probably be more helpful than ever in finding a good job.
(4) Ability to use computers will be the single most important factor in finding a good job.
(5) Factories again will be hiring more workers.

17. Which of the following statements expresses an opinion from the passage, rather than a fact?

(1) Between 1980 and 1986 the number of factory jobs decreased by about 2 million.
(2) The decline in manufacturing jobs is a sure sign that America's economy is in serious trouble.
(3) Between 1980 and 1986 the overall unemployment rate in America decreased.
(4) The number of service jobs has been increasing.
(5) Professional, managerial, and technical sector jobs generally require training and the ability to work with information.

Item 18 is based on the following graphs.

JOB PAY, 1984

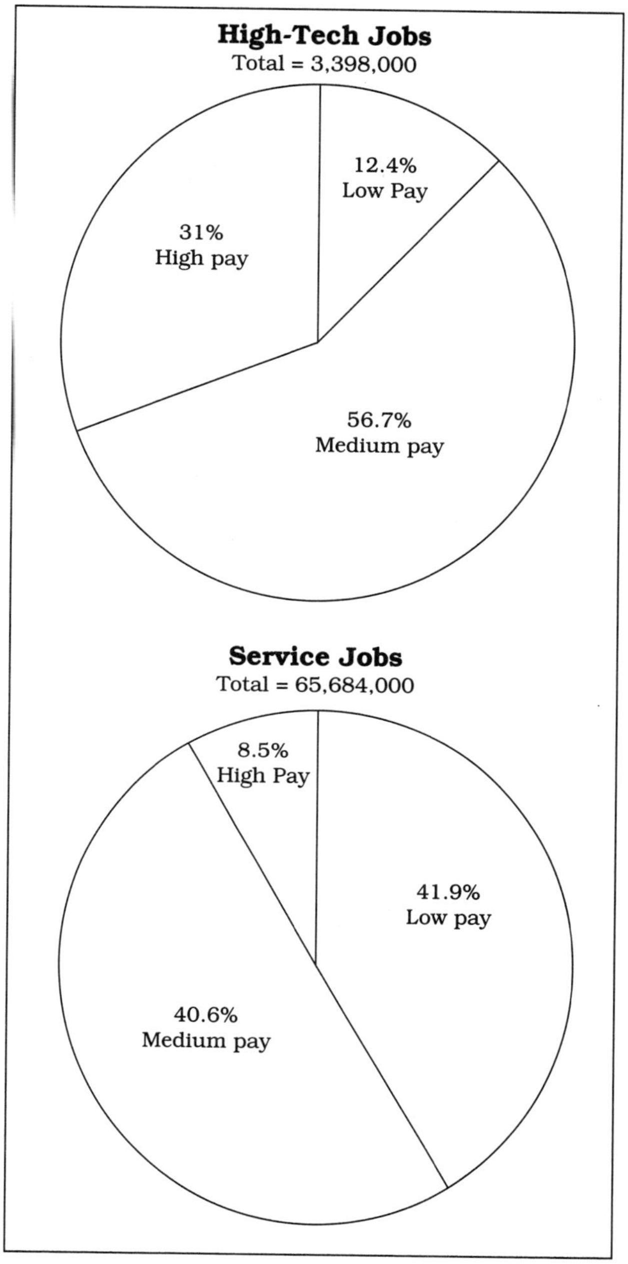

18. Which of the following statements is clearly supported by the graphs?

(1) Most new jobs created today are high-tech or service jobs.

(2) There are far more low-paying service jobs than there are low-paying high-tech jobs.

(3) The majority of the nation's high-paying jobs are high-tech jobs.

(4) High-tech jobs, but not service jobs, require a college education.

(5) The average pay for service jobs and high-tech jobs is similar.

Items 19 and 20 are based on the following information.

In the fall of 1987 skirt hemlines rose again. The clothing industry hoped consumers would like the new look. If not, the industry, which had invested a lot of money in the short skirts, could be seriously hurt. But the industry felt it had to take the risk. Sales in recent years had been slow. Consumers had been spending relatively little money on clothes. If the new skirt length caught on, many women would feel the clothes they owned were out of date. And they'd be buying lots of clothes once again.

19. Clothing manufacturers introduced shorter skirts because

(1) consumers wanted the shorter skirts
(2) long skirts seemed old-fashioned and impractical
(3) the manufacturers wanted to increase sales
(4) the manufacturers were afraid to take any risks
(5) the manufacturers wanted to be different from their competitors

20. Which of the following statements about the relationship between consumers and manufacturers is suggested by the passage?

(1) Consumers will purchase whatever manufacturers produce.
(2) Manufacturers have no influence on consumer tastes and preferences.
(3) Manufacturers have some influence on consumer tastes, but this influence has its limits.
(4) Manufacturers are not concerned about whether or not consumers will buy their products.
(5) Manufacturers' decisions on what to produce are based entirely on what consumers have said they want to buy.

Items 21 to 24 are based on the following table.

Percentage of Income Spent for Rent, New York City, 1984

Household Income	Total Households (in thousands)	Percentage of Households in an Income Group That Paid Rent of More Than 25% of income	40% of income
\$ 0—\$ 3,999	143	100.0%	91.6%
\$ 4,000—\$ 9,999	609	91.5%	64.5%
\$ 10,000—\$12,449	185	81.6%	31.4%
\$ 12,500—\$14,449	113	69.0%	15.0%
\$ 14,500—\$19,999	232	45.6%	6.9%
\$ 20,000—\$24,999	182	28.6%	3.3%
\$ 25,000—\$34,999	208	14.4%	1.0%
\$ 35,000 OR MORE	228	7.9%	0.9%
All Renter Households	1,900	60.2%	32.9%

21. Based on the table, which of the following is a true statement about renter households in New York City in 1984?

(1) Most households had an income of \$35,000 or more.
(2) Most households spent over half of their income on rent.
(3) About one-third of all households spent more than 40 percent of their income on rent.
(4) Many households in the lowest (\$0—\$3,999) bracket spent their entire income on rent.
(5) In the \$14,500—\$19,999 income bracket, over three-quarters of all households spent less than 25% percent of their income on rent.

22. A full picture of what portions of their incomes New York City residents spent on housing would be made up of the data in the table and data on

(1) the size of welfare payments for the poor
(2) the costs of housing for home owners in relation to income
(3) the population of poor people in New York City
(4) the cost of construction of new housing in New York City
(5) the size of the average household in New York City

23. Which of the following statements is a generalization based on the findings in the table?

(1) Housing is a minor part of most renters' expenses in New York City.
(2) The lower the household income, the greater the portion of that income that is devoted to rent.
(3) Rents are the single largest expense for New Yorkers at all levels of income.
(4) Rents in New York City are higher than rents in most other urban areas.
(5) The high cost of rent in New York has encouraged many New York employers to pay their employees higher salaries.

24. Which of the following policy recommendations for the City of New York is most directly suggested by data in the table?

(1) More must be done to help the homeless.
(2) More affordable housing is needed for low-income residents.
(3) New methods should be developed for resolving problems that arise between landlords and tenants.
(4) The pace of construction in New York City should be slowed down.
(5) Mass transit service to many neighborhoods needs to be improved.

Items 25 to 30 are based on the following information.

There are several different kinds of credit cards. The three main kinds are (1) gas company and retail store credit cards, (2) bank credit cards, like Mastercard and Visa, and (3) "travel and entertainment" cards like American Express. Each kind of card has its advantages and disadvantages.

Retail store cards and gas company cards are the easiest to obtain. Also, consumers find it useful to have credit with the businesses they most rely on. In 1986, $63 billion was charged on retail store cards, and $21 billion was charged on gas company cards. There is no annual fee connected with using these cards. But the interest charged on money owed is very high—as much as 21 percent.

Bank cards are somewhat more difficult to obtain. But they have the advantage of being accepted by many businesses, rather than just one company. Another advantage is that different bank cards have different terms regarding interest rates and annual fees. So consumers have more of a chance of finding a card that's right for their particular needs. Some bank cards involve high annual fees but relatively low interest on money owned. Others involve higher interest charges but relatively low annual fees. All bank cards, however, have a spending limit. A person can't charge more than his or her limit. In 1986, $144 billion was charged on bank cards.

Travel and entertainment (T&E) cards are usually the most difficult to obtain. There is usually a high annual charge for a T&E card. However, there is no spending limit or interest charge. All charges must be paid off at the end of each month. Payments may not be spread out. In 1986, $63 million was charged on T&E cards.

25. Which of the following is an advantage of retail store credit cards?

(1) No interest is charged.
(2) Very low interest is charged.
(3) The cards are not difficult to get.
(4) The cards can be used in a wide range of businesses.
(5) Interest rates and fees charged vary considerably.

26. A consumer wants a card that will allow her to spread out payments on purchases. But she also wants to keep her interest payments down. What kind of card should she be advised to apply for?

(1) a retail store card
(2) any bank card
(3) a bank card with low interest rate
(4) a bank card with a low annual fee
(5) a travel and entertainment card

27. For which of the following individuals would a T&E card probably be most useful?

(1) John is working in his first job and wants to apply for a credit card that won't be too hard to get.
(2) James does most of his shopping at one store and would like to have credit with that store.
(3) Mary has some major purchases to make and wants to be able to pay them off over time.
(4) Paul does work that requires him to spend large sums of money but enables him to pay the money off immediately.
(5) Susan travels a lot in connection with her work and wants to be able to pay for her gas with credit.

28. Which of the following statements is <u>not</u> supported by the information?

(1) Some types of credit cards have a wide range of uses; others are more limited in their uses.
(2) Some types of credit cards are given to anyone who applies; others are not.
(3) Some types of credit cards have spending limits; others do not.
(4) Some types of credit cards have annual fees; others do not.
(5) Some types of credit cards require payment each month; others allow payment over time.

29. The bulk of the 1986 credit charges were made on

(1) travel and entertainment cards
(2) department store cards
(3) Visa credit cards
(4) Bank credit cards
(5) retail store and oil company credit cards

30. Edna wants the use of credit cards, but she wants never to pay out any more money than the cost of the articles she purchases. Edna should use

(1) bank and retail store cards
(2) bank and T&E cards
(3) bank and gas company cards
(4) retail store and gas company cards
(5) retail store and T&E cards

Answers are on pages 130–133.

Political Science Items

Directions: Choose the one best answer for each question.

Items 1 to 3 are based on the following information.

To measure public opinion, political scientists look at many different factors. The following are five such factors.

(1) stability—how long an opinion on an issue lasts
(2) latency—whether an opinion on an issue has already been clearly formed or is still only a tentative, possible opinion
(3) intensity—how strongly an opinion on an issue is held
(4) salience—the extent to which people personally identify with the issue involved
(5) polarization—the extent to which voters as a whole are united or divided on an issue

1. A public opinion pollster asks you, "Since when have you supported affirmative action programs?" Which of the following factors is being measured?

(1) stability
(2) intensity
(3) latency
(4) salience
(5) polarization

2. A public opinion pollster asks you, "How deeply are you personally involved in the nuclear freeze movement?" Which of the following factors is being measured?

(1) stability
(2) intensity
(3) latency
(4) salience
(5) polarization

3. A poll shows that a solid majority of the public supports gun control laws. Which of the following factors did it measure?

(1) stability
(2) intensity
(3) latency
(4) salience
(5) polarization

4. After World War II the United States developed a policy of containment toward the Soviet Union. This policy said the United States should prevent Soviet expansion by resisting Soviet demands and by militarily and economically strengthening the nations of the free world.
Which of the following actions by the United States would best illustrate an application of the containment policy?

(1) cutting back on foreign aid to free world nations
(2) negotiating with the Soviet Union on limiting nuclear arms
(3) establishing a military alliance with other free world nations
(4) increasing exports to reduce America's balance of trade deficit
(5) taking a less active role in foreign affairs

Items 5 and 6 are based on the following information.

Special-interest groups (groups representing labor, business, farmers, supporters or opponents of gun control, etc.) often hire lobbyists to present their points of view to Congress. Lobbyists try to persuade Congresspeople to pass bills that will be favorable to the group they represent. Lobbyists provide Congresspeople with data and sometimes even write bills to be introduced. To ensure that lobbyists do not give special-interest groups too big a say, there are laws that regulate their activities.

5. Which of the following statements expresses an opinion, rather than a fact, about lobbyists?

(1) A wide range of groups are represented by lobbyists.
(2) Lobbyists try to influence the laws that are made.
(3) Lobbyists are sometimes involved in the writing of legislation.
(4) Lobbyists have had a harmful effect on the political system by giving a big say to special-interest groups.
(5) Today there are laws that regulate lobbyists and the activities that they engage in.

6. Which of the following statements could be used to argue in favor of lobbyists and lobbying?

(1) Lobbyists are known to use tactics such as gifts and bribes.
(2) Laws regulating lobbying activities have so far not proven effective.
(3) Lobbyists can often give congresspeople an informed view of complicated issues.
(4) The views that lobbyists present of issues are often somewhat slanted to one side of the issue.
(5) The lobbying process may cause politicians to lose sight of the views of the average citizen.

Item 7 is based on the following graph.

SOURCES OF FEDERAL INCOME, 1986*
Total income: $794 billion

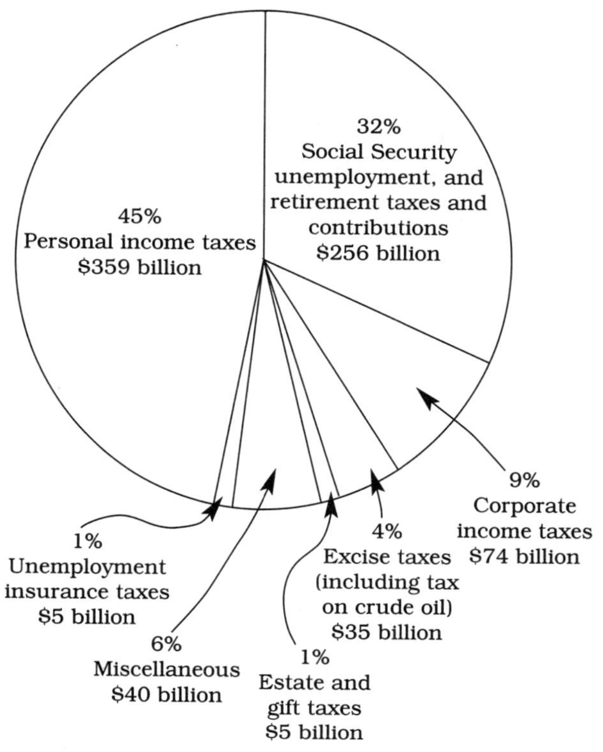

*Figures are based on estimates

7. Which statement is supported by information in the graph?

(1) Income taxes provide over half of the government's income.

(2) The government's income is not enough to cover its expenses.

(3) Government income has nearly doubled over the last decade.

(4) The government gets most of its income by taxing corporations.

(5) The United States has more kinds of taxes than most other Western nations.

Items 8 and 9 are based on the following graphs.

U.S. FOREIGN AID, 1987

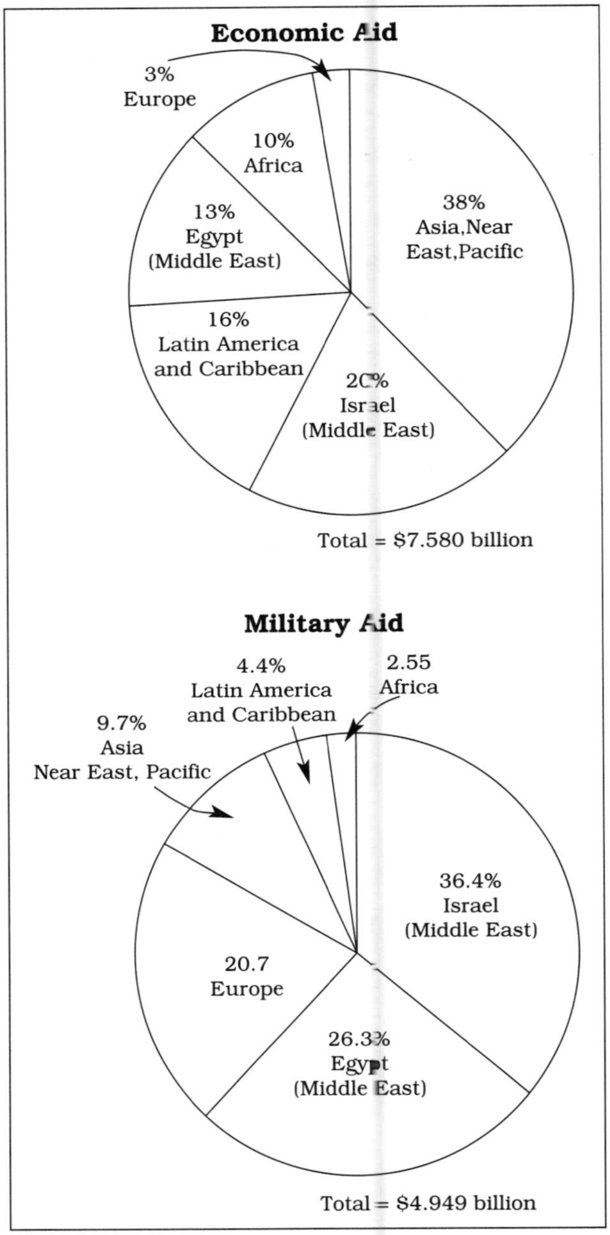

8. Based on the graphs, it can be concluded that U.S. foreign policy

(1) focuses more on military issues than on economic issues
(2) has been shaped mainly by ideological conflict with Asia
(3) regards the Middle East as being an area of considerable importance
(4) centers on the need to protect U.S. borders and ensure stability in the rest of the Western hemisphere
(5) has since World War II focused on building Western Europe's economy

9. Which of the following is <u>not</u> true?

(1) Asia, the Near East, and the Pacific receive more economic aid than military aid.
(2) Latin America and the Caribbean receive more military aid than economic aid.
(3) Compared to other parts of the world Africa receives relatively little aid from the United States.
(4) Europe receives more military aid than do Asia, the Near East, and the Pacific.
(5) Israel receives one-fifth of U.S. economic aid.

Item 10 is based on the following cartoon.

—from *Herblock At Large* (Pantheon Books, 1987)

10. In the cartoon, the speaker is telling the graduating class that

(1) a career in government leads to a high salary
(2) there is the opportunity for corruption in government
(3) anyone in the U.S. may someday become president
(4) there are many job openings in government
(5) anyone working in government needs to study economics

11. The federal government uses several types of grants in giving money to states and local governments. Different types of grants have different conditions. With categorical grants, for example, states must use the money for a specific purpose, must submit plans to the federal government for approval, and must allow the federal government to supervise how the money is spent. With revenue-sharing grants, on the other hand, the federal government sets only very general conditions. States may pretty much use the money as they choose.

Which of the following statements is best supported by the information?

(1) Categorical grants usually involve more money than revenue-sharing grants.
(2) Categorical grants give the federal government more control over the money that is given out than revenue-sharing grants do.
(3) Only some states are eligible for revenue-sharing whereas all are eligible for categorical grants.
(4) Federal spending cuts have hurt categorical grants more than they have revenue-sharing grants.
(5) Categorical grants give states a larger say over how to spend the money received than do revenue-sharing grants.

Items 12 and 13 are based on the following diagram.

TWO FORMS OF CITY GOVERNMENT

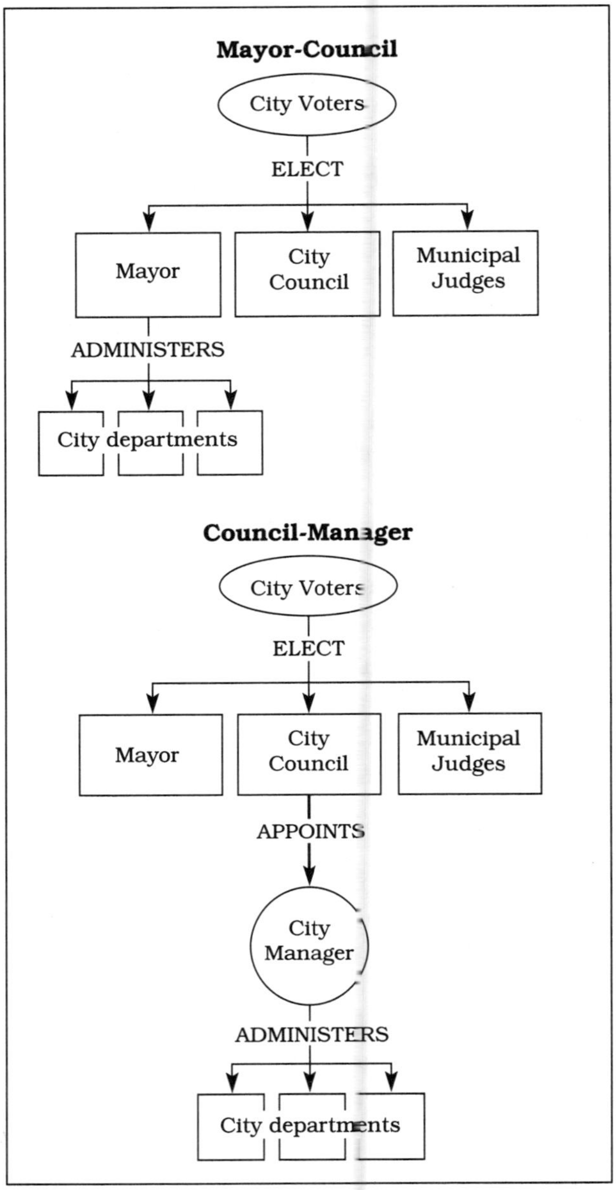

12. The main difference between the mayor-council and council-manager forms of city government is that

(1) in the mayor-council form the city council has no powers
(2) in the mayor-council form there are fewer city departments
(3) in the mayor-council form there is no city manager
(4) in the council-manager form there is no mayor
(5) in the council-manager form municipal judges have fewer powers

13. It has been said that voters in cities with a council-manager form of government have less power than voters in cities with a mayor-council form of government. Which of the following statements explains why?

(1) The council-manager form of government is a much newer system than the mayor-council form.
(2) Cities have much larger budgets today than they had in the past.
(3) In both the mayor-council and council-manager forms of government, voters elect a mayor, city council members, and municipal judges.
(4) In the council-manager form of government, city departments are administered by an appointed official rather than an elected official.
(5) The city manager in the council-manager form of government is often a person with special training in city administration and urban affairs.

Items 14 and 15 are based on the following quote.

"I continue to maintain, as in 1945, that on ideology there is no prospect of compromise between the [Soviet Union] and ourselves, but that we must find ways to settle as many areas as possible in order to live together on this small planet without war."

—1975, W. Averill Harriman
(former U.S. ambassador to the Soviet Union)

14. In 1975 W. Averill Harriman evidently believed that

(1) war between the U.S. and the Soviet Union has become unavoidable
(2) the U.S. and the Soviet Union have similar ideologies
(3) the U.S. and the Soviet Union can and should cooperate on a range of issues
(4) the U.S. economy would be strengthened significantly if the United States adopted the Soviet political and economic system
(5) world peace will be possible only when the U.S. has militarily defeated the Soviet Union

15. Which of the following actions by the United States would best carry out Harriman's recommendation?

(1) sell weapons to countries that are enemies of the Soviet Union
(2) boycott sports competitions the Soviet Union participates in
(3) impose restrictions on imports from the Soviet Union
(4) impose restrictions on exports to the Soviet Union
(5) negotiate a mutual arms reduction agreement with the Soviet Union

Item 16 is based on the following cartoon.

Dennis Renault, *Sacramento Bee*. By permission of the cartoonist.

16. Which of the following best states the point the cartoon makes?

(1) The United Nations has consistently supported American policies toward Israel.
(2) The United States is the major benefactor of the United Nations.
(3) The American public's faith in the United Nations has increased in recent years.
(4) The United States has lost some of its power to persuade and lead other nations in the United Nations.
(5) Within the United Nations the United States has more influence in the General Assembly than in the Security Council.

Items 17 and 18 are based on the following map.

U.S. TREATY COMMITMENTS

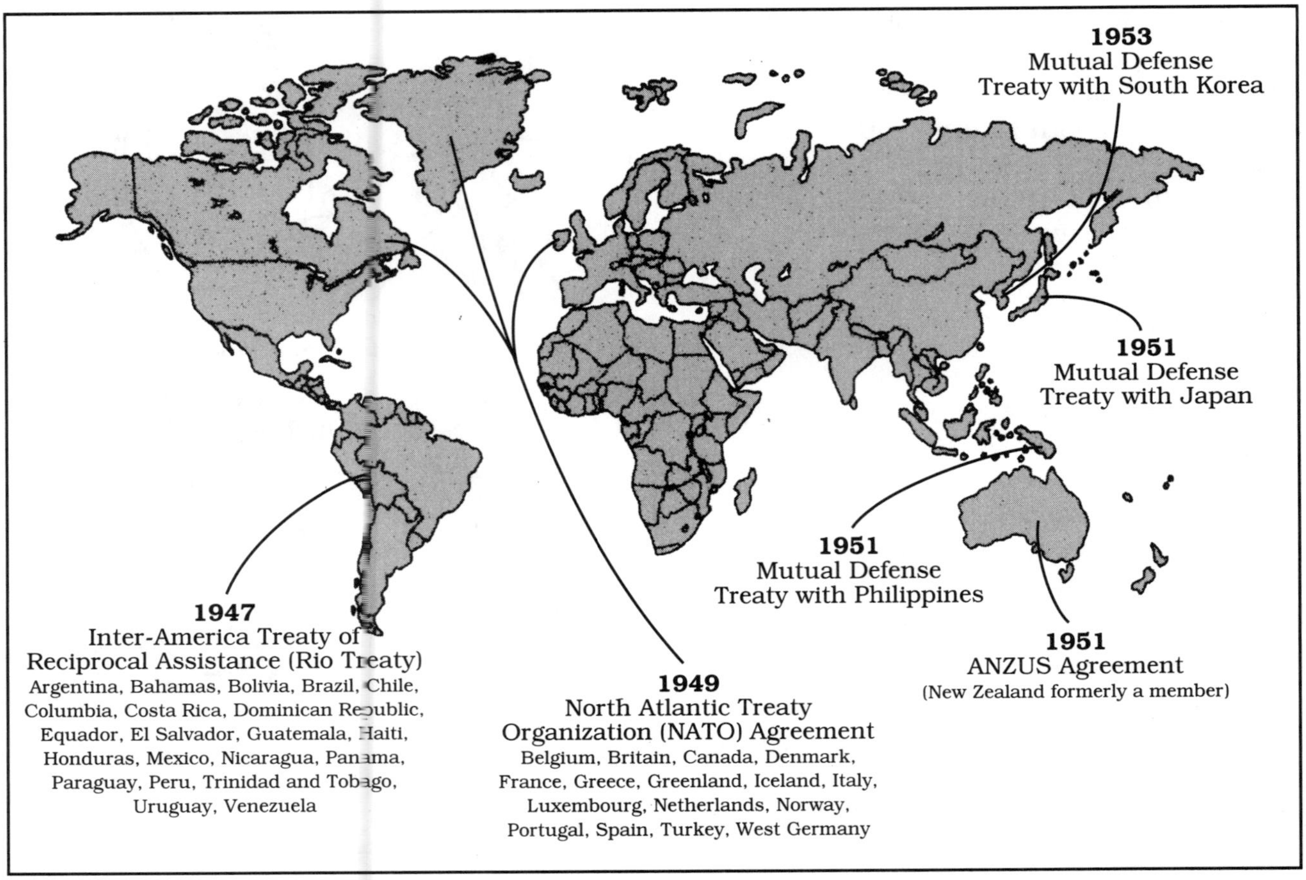

17. The primary purpose of most of the treaties shown on the map is to

(1) establish trading partners for the United States
(2) ensure friendly relations between the United States and its neighbors
(3) ease tensions between the United States and the former Soviet Union
(4) commit the United States and its allies to militarily defend one another
(5) enable people in the countries that signed to become more familiar with one another's cultures

18. Which of the following statements about the treaties shown in the map is supported by information in the map?

(1) The treaties were signed in the cold war period following World War II.
(2) The treaties each involve the United States and a group of other countries.
(3) Most of the treaties are no longer in effect.
(4) The treaties establish U.S. military bases around the world and foreign bases in the United States.
(5) The treaties involve countries in every continent.

Items 19 to 22 are based on the following information.

Foreign policies can be classified according to the ways nations interact with each other. Listed below are five types of foreign policy and brief descriptions of each.

(1) imperialism—a country assumes long-term control of another country for purposes of its own prestige, economic benefit, or military gain
(2) internationalism—a country joins alliances, regional associations, and world organizations and respects the interests and needs of other nations
(3) interventionism—a country temporarily interferes in the domestic affairs of another country to change that country's government, restore order, or help the government in power
(4) isolationism—a country avoids political and economic alliances with other countries and stays out of regional and world organizations
(5) neutralism—a country participates in international organizations but refuses to side with rival powers

Each of the following descriptions is an example of one of the foreign policies described above. Choose the foreign policy type that best fits the description. The types may be used more than once in the set of items. No one question has more than one best answer.

19. At the end of World War I the government of the United States refused to join the newly created world organization known as the League of Nations and refused to become involved in the disputes or conflicts of other nations. This foreign policy is an example of

(1) imperialism
(2) internationalism
(3) interventionism
(4) isolationism
(5) neutralism

20. From the 1800s until 1947 Great Britain ruled India through royal governors and British officials. Britain established exclusive trading rights for itself, stationed British troops on Indian soil, and ensured that British citizens in India received preferred treatment. This foreign policy is an example of

(1) imperialism
(2) internationalism
(3) interventionism
(4) isolationism
(5) neutralism

21. Egypt has determined to chart its own course in the Middle East and the world. A member of the United Nations, Egypt has been interested in Arab affairs but has not sided exclusively with either the Asian or American camps. This foreign policy is an example of

(1) imperialism
(2) internationalism
(3) interventionism
(4) isolationism
(5) neutralism

22. The United States has joined the Organization of American States and the North Atlantic Treaty Organization, two major regional and defensive associations of Western nations. It has also signed mutual assistance treaties with Taiwan and a number of other countries and is a founding member of the United Nations. This foreign policy is an example of

(1) imperialism
(2) internationalism
(3) interventionism
(4) isolationism
(5) neutralism

Item 23 is based on the following chart.

Qualifications for Election to Congress

Requirement	House of Representatives	Senate
Age	At least 25 years old	At least 30 years old
Citizenship	U.S. citizen for at least 7 years	U.S. citizen for at least 9 years
Residence	Resident of state in which elected	Resident of state he or she represents

23. Based on the information, which of the following individuals would be eligible to run for senator in California?

(1) a twenty-eight-year-old man who has been a U.S. citizen for eight years and lives in California
(2) a fifty-year-old man who has been a U.S. citizen his entire life and resides in Nevada
(3) a thirty-four-year-old woman who has been a U.S. citizen for ten years and resides in California
(4) a twenty-year-old woman who lives in California and recently became a citizen
(5) a forty-year-old woman who was born in California, has been a U.S. citizen her entire life, and now resides in New York

24. Judicial review refers to the power of the judiciary to review state and federal laws as well as executive acts in order to determine whether these laws and acts are in keeping with the U.S. Constitution. If a law or act is found unconstitutional, it is void and has no legal force.

Which of the following is an example of judicial review?

(1) The Senate reviews the qualifications of a judge that the president has nominated to fill a Supreme Court vacancy.
(2) Congress impeaches a judge for misconduct in office.
(3) The Supreme Court rules that a law is a violation of the First Amendment.
(4) Congress proposes an amendment to the Constitution, and this amendment is then ratified by the states.
(5) A legal decision made by a lower court may be reviewed by a higher court.

Items 25 and 26 are based on the following diagram.

HOW THE CONSTITUTION DIVIDES POWER BETWEEN THE FEDERAL GOVERNMENT AND THE STATES

POWERS OF THE FEDERAL GOVERNMENT	SHARED POWERS	POWERS OF STATE GOVERNMENTS
1. To conduct foreign relations 2. To declare war 3. To regulate interstate and foreign commerce 4. To regulate immigration and establish laws permitting naturalization 5. To raise and maintain armed forces 6. To govern territories and admit new states 7. To print and coin money 8. To establish post offices and post roads 9. To grant patents and copyrights 10. To make all laws "necessary and proper" to carry out its constitutional responsibilities	1. To levy and collect taxes 2. To borrow money 3. To establish superior and inferior courts 4. To enforce laws 5. To apprehend and punish lawbreakers 6. To charter banks and other corporations 7. To take land for public use 8. To provide for the general welfare	1. To regulate trade within the state 2. To establish local governments 3. To protect the public health, safety, and morals 4. To ratify constitutional amendments 5. To create laws regulating marriage and divorce 6. To conduct elections 7. To change state constitutions and the form of state and local governments 8. To establish and support public schools 9. To license various occupational specialties 10. To exercise the "reserved powers" not granted to the federal government nor prohibited to the states

25. Which of the following statements can be explained by the division of power shown in the diagram?

(1) Individuals pay both federal and state taxes.
(2) State constitutions are often easier to amend than the federal Constitution.
(3) Like the president, most state governors serve four-year terms.
(4) Like the national legislature, most state legislatures have two houses.
(5) In the twentieth century there has been a trend toward more federal power and less state power.

26. States are able to do all of the following except

(1) open a system of public colleges
(2) sign a trade agreement with a foreign country
(3) create and maintain a licensing procedure for doctors
(4) try people who are suspected of having committed a crime
(5) set aside land for use as park land

27. The President's powers are mainly executive. But the Constitution also gives the President some quasi-judicial powers—powers connected with the courts and the administration of justice. For example, the President has the power to nominate federal judges.

Which of the following Presidential activities provides another example of quasi-judicial powers?

(1) accepting or rejecting legislation proposed by Congress
(2) negotiating treaties with other nations
(3) serving as commander-in-chief of the armed forces
(4) granting pardons to suspected or convicted criminals
(5) supervising government employees

Items 28 to 30 are based on the following information.

An important part of the American heritage is two different but related concepts of freedom: negative freedom and positive freedom.

The idea of negative freedom arose during the colonial period. The colonists felt that the British government was making unreasonable demands and that citizens should be free from such demands. Negative freedom, then, is the idea that government may not interfere in certain aspects of citizens' lives because to do so would be an abuse of power. Negative freedom can be thought of as "freedom from." For example, the government may not arrest people who criticize its policies: People are free from arrest for expressing their political beliefs.

But Americans soon learned that negative freedom was not enough. They developed the idea of positive freedom, or "freedom to" be able to act. Positive freedom removes obstacles that prevent people from doing something or gives people the means to act. For example, an extension of voting rights gives people the means to participate in government. It is therefore an example of "freedom to" or positive freedom.

28. Which of the following statements is best supported by the passage?

(1) Freedom means that a country has no rules or regulations.
(2) It is impossible for a country to have negative and positive freedom.
(3) Positive freedom is an older concept than negative freedom.
(4) Positive freedom is a more important concept than negative freedom.
(5) Our laws have been shaped by ideas of negative and positive freedom.

29. Which of the following statements offers the best example of positive freedom?

(1) The government may not interfere with people holding a meeting for a peaceful purpose.
(2) Government leaders are prevented from arresting opposition politicians who criticize their policies.
(3) The United States government is not allowed to establish an official religion and force citizens to support it.
(4) Citizens may petition government to right wrongs that have caused them to suffer.
(5) Public officials are prohibited from banning newspaper stories before they are published.

30. Which of the following amendments to the Constitution is the best example of negative freedom?

(1) Eighth Amendment, restricting judges from setting excessive bail and fines or imposing cruel and unusual punishments
(2) Fourteenth Amendment, granting citizenship to former slaves
(3) Seventeenth Amendment, letting people vote directly for their United States senators
(4) Nineteenth Amendment, giving women the right to vote in national elections
(5) Twenty-fourth Amendment, lowering the voting age to eighteen

Answers are on pages 133–135.

Behavioral Science Items

Directions: Choose the one best answer for each question.

Item 1 is based on the following table.

Percent of Firearms Usage in Selected Crimes, by Region, 1985

Region	Murder	Assault	Robbery
Northeast	50.9	13.5	28.3
Midwest	60.7	22.2	37.2
South	63.1	25.4	41.7
West	54.3	19.9	35.1
U.S. Total	58.7	21.3	35.3

Source: U.S. Federal Bureau of Investigation

1. Which of the following statements is supported by the table?

(1) The Northeast shows the lowest rates of firearms usage for all three types of crimes.
(2) The Midwest shows the highest rates of firearms usage for all three types of crimes.
(3) In all regions firearms are more likely to be used in assaults than in robberies.
(4) The West has more privately owned firearms than any of the other regions.
(5) Rates of firearms usage have risen sharply in all regions, and particularly in the South.

Items 2 and 3 refer to the following passage.

For the Polynesian a taboo is a strong prohibition against touching, saying, or doing something because of fear of punishment from a superhuman force. An act or object that is taboo gives rise to feelings of horror mixed with disgust.

Social scientists have borrowed the term "taboo" to describe behaviors that are forbidden, even though they may not be illegal. For example, most societies have a taboo against incest even though they may not have laws against incest.

2. Which of the following claims is supported by the information?

(1) All societies have the same taboos.
(2) The laws of a society define what is taboo in that society.
(3) Taboo behaviors are less likely to occur than behaviors that are not taboo.
(4) There are no taboos in modern American society.
(5) The rulers of a society decide what taboos the society will have.

3. The social science term "taboo" is like the original Polynesian concept in that both

(1) focus on incest
(2) involve religion and the supernatural
(3) describe prohibitions that are not based on law
(4) were developed centuries ago
(5) apply to children more than to adults

Items 4 to 7 are based on the following information.

People have different grounds for making moral judgments. Psychologist Lawrence Kohlberg has classified the grounds people use to make moral decisions by several different "orientations." Following are brief descriptions of five of those orientations for making judgments about right and wrong.

(1) punishment and obedience—judgments are based on how the authorities will respond to an act: positively or negatively
(2) good boy/nice girl—judgments are based on the opinions of other people
(3) law-and-order—judgments are based on laws and on following the law
(4) social contract/legalistic—judgments are based on concern for individuals and the well-being of the community
(5) conscience—judgments are based on one's own values and principles of right and wrong

Kohlberg developed his classification system by asking people to give him their judgments of right and wrong in response to various moral dilemmas. Consider this typical one:

A woman was near death from a rare disease. The one drug that could save her was manufactured only by a local druggist. The drug was expensive to make. Since he was the only supplier, the druggist realized he could make a tremendous profit, so he charged customers ten times the drug's cost. The woman's husband was unable to raise enough money. He begged the druggist to sell him the drug for less money. The druggist refused. Becoming desperate, the husband broke into the store and stole the drug.

The following statements are four different answers to the question, "Should the husband have stolen the drug?" Choose the orientation that the answer best fits. The orientations may be used more than once in the set of items. No one question has more than one best answer.

4. "The husband was right; the one who was in the wrong was the druggist. No one would blame the husband for what he did." This response is an example of

(1) punishment and obedience
(2) good boy/nice girl
(3) law-and-order
(4) social contract/legalistic
(5) conscience

5. "In my system of values, a person's life is more important than anything else. For this reason I believe that breaking into a store is right if it's the only way to save a life." This response is an example of

(1) punishment and obedience
(2) good boy/nice girl
(3) law-and-order
(4) social contract/legalistic
(5) conscience

6. "That husband shouldn't have done what he did. Stealing is something you can get put in jail for." This response is an example of

(1) punishment and obedience
(2) good boy/nice girl
(3) law-and-order
(4) social contract/legalistic
(5) conscience

7. "I feel sorry for the husband. He was in a tough situation. But the law is the law, and he shouldn't have broken it. So I guess I'd have to say he did the wrong thing." This response is an example of

(1) punishment and obedience
(2) good boy/nice girl
(3) law-and-order
(4) social contract/legalistic
(5) conscience

Item 8 is based on the following cartoon.

——from *Herblock on All Fronts* (New American Library, 1980)

8. The problem shown in the cartoon could be addressed most directly by

(1) opening more schools in crowded districts
(2) placing less emphasis on college preparation work
(3) introducing more science into the school curriculum
(4) establishing tougher standards in schools
(5) making the school curriculum less demanding

Items 9 and 10 are based on the following information.

Cultures generally have strong ideas about the differences between men and women. But interestingly, different cultures have very different ideas. For example, in American culture men have traditionally been considered to be practical and unemotional; women, to be sensitive and emotional. Iranians, however, have just the opposite idea: They consider women to be practical and men to be emotional. We accept, and encourage, emotional behavior in women but not in men. Iranians accept and encourage such behavior in men but not in women.

9. Which of the following best states the main idea of the passage?

(1) Each individual has a unique personality.
(2) Different cultures consider different personality traits to be typical of men and women.
(3) Traits that Americans associate with men are associated with women in Iran.
(4) The different cultures of the world have little in common with each other.
(5) Men and women should be treated equally.

10. Which of the following hypotheses is best supported by the information?

(1) Personality differences between men and women are caused by biological differences.
(2) Personality differences between men and women may be influenced by cultural factors.
(3) There are fewer differences between men and women as people grow older.
(4) Most cultures think the way Americans do about the differences between men and women.
(5) The differences between men and women have been the same throughout history.

Item 11 is based on the following table.

Poverty Rate by Age Group
(in percentages)

Age	Rate (% of population)
Less than 15	21.5
15–24	16.6
25–44	10.6
45–54	8.4
55–59	9.8
60–64	11.3
65 and over	12.6

11. From the poverty rate figures in the chart you could conclude that there is a particularly urgent need for employment and skills training programs for

(1) recent college graduates
(2) immigrants from other countries
(3) people in economically depressed areas of the country
(4) parents of young children
(5) retirees on fixed incomes

Item 12 is based on the following graph

ILLINOIS' ELDERLY POPULATION*

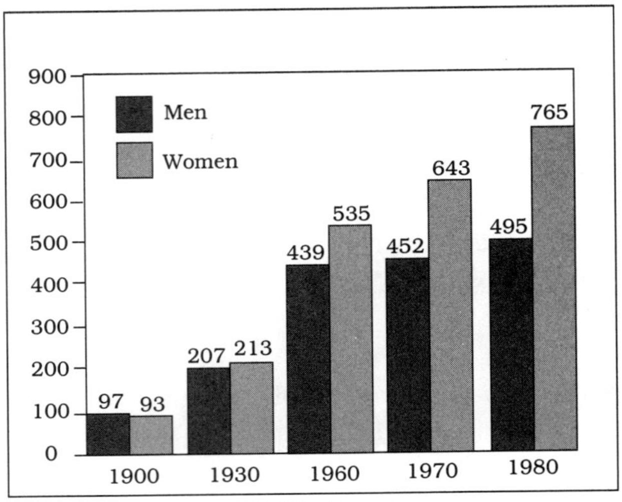

*Information based on 1980 U.S. Census

12. Which of the following statements is best supported by the figure?

(1) Older people tend to leave Illinois and settle in other states.
(2) Illinois has a larger proportion of elderly people than most other states.
(3) Life expectancy in Illinois decreased over the period shown.
(4) Life expectancy in Illinois is greater for women than for men.
(5) Women in Illinois tend to work fewer years than men do.

13. Psychologists studied the performance of about 40 baseball pitchers over a period of six years. These pitchers were talented players who began with one-year contracts but hoped to obtain long-term contracts. The psychologists found that the pitchers' performance improved steadily until they were awarded long-term contracts. Once the pitchers had long-term contracts, their performance worsened.

Which of the following conclusions is supported by the research findings?

(1) Performance is affected by how motivated a person is.

(2) Performance depends exclusively on how much talent a person has.

(3) Performance of individuals varies from year to year in unpredictable ways.

(4) Performance tends to get worse over time.

(5) Performance is a matter of how much experience a person has.

Item 14 refers to the following table.

Enrollment of Exceptional Children in Special Programs, 1932 to 1975*

Year	Total
1975	7,886,000
1970	3,158,000
1966	2,106,000
1963	1,682,000
1958	890,000
1953	497,000
1948	378,000
1940	314,000
1936	297,000
1932	164,000

* Programs are for students considered handicapped, learning disabled, or gifted.

From U.S. Department of the Census (1975), with 1970 data based on state reports to the U.S. Office of Education and 1975 data from the Statistical Abstract of the U.S., 1976

14. Which of the following statements is best supported by the table?

(1) The largest category of students in special programs are the learning disabled.

(2) The first programs for exceptional children were begun in 1932.

(3) Programs for exceptional children received much more attention in the 1960s and 1970s than they had from the 1930s-1950s.

(4) By 1975 there were enough special programs in schools to meet the needs of most exceptional children.

(5) Since 1975 there has been a movement away from special programs, so that most exceptional children are now placed in regular classes.

Items 15 and 16 are based on the following information.

Delayed gratification means deliberately sacrificing immediate desires for the sake of long-term goals. Learning to delay gratification is a necessary step in achieving self-control.

15. Which of the following statements follows logically from the information?

(1) Children are incapable of delayed gratification.
(2) The tendency to sacrifice immediate desires leads to deep psychological problems.
(3) People with self-control are able to delay gratification.
(4) Individuals who delay gratification usually act on impulse.
(5) Most people don't have any long-term goals.

16. Which of the following best exemplifies delayed gratification?

(1) going to a party instead of studying for an exam
(2) changing from one job to another
(3) working overtime and saving the money for school
(4) taking an earned vacation
(5) taking a week off from work because of sickness

Items 17 to 20 refer to the following information.

In big cities, psychologists have argued, people feel anonymous–like they're "faces in the crowd." And this feeling leads them to do things they would otherwise not do.

To test this hypothesis, psychologists observed reactions to an abandoned car in New York City and in a small California town. The car in the California town was left for a week without a part being stolen or vandalized. In contrast, the car in New York City began to be stripped ten minutes after it was abandoned. By the end of the first day, every removable part was gone; in the first three days, there were 23 incidents of destruction.

Much of the vandalism, psychologists found, was committed not by teenagers, but by adults. The adults were all well dressed and appeared to be mature, responsible citizens.

17. Which of the following best states the hypothesis the researchers were testing?

(1) Vandalism has become an accepted part of modern life in America.
(2) The feeling of being unknown and unrecognized leads people to act in ways they themselves might not approve of.
(3) There are considerable differences between the East Coast and the West Coast when it comes to moral standards.
(4) Teenagers of today have rebelled against the moral standards of adults and are more likely to commit acts of destruction.
(5) The feeling of anonymity in big cities often leads people to feelings of loneliness and despair.

18. What was the result of the psychologists' experiment?

(1) The hypothesis was disproved by the fact that the car in California wasn't vandalized.
(2) The hypothesis was disproved by the speed with which the vandalism occurred in New York.
(3) The hypothesis was supported by the fact that vandalism occurred in New York but not California, but contradicted by the fact that the vandals were well-dressed adults and not teenagers.
(4) The hypothesis was supported by the fact that the vandals were well-dressed adults, but contradicted by the fact that vandalism occurred in New York and not in California.
(5) The hypothesis was supported by the fact that vandalism occurred in New York but not California, and by the fact that the vandals were well-dressed adults.

19. Which of the following conclusions is best supported by the experiment?

(1) Different environments have different effects on people's behavior.
(2) Anonymity has positive and negative effects on people's behavior.
(3) Small towns have eliminated crime.
(4) Small towns are better places to live than big cities.
(5) Crime in cities usually takes the form of vandalism.

20. A hypothesis can't be proven on the basis of a single experiment. Social scientists typically conduct additional experiments to further confirm—or disprove—the hypothesis. In the case of the present study, which of the following would <u>not</u> be useful as a further test of the hypothesis?

(1) The same experiment is repeated in a different neighborhood of New York City and a small New York State town.
(2) Wallets containing identification and a large sum of money are "dropped" in a large city and a small town, and the return rate is observed.
(3) The original experiment is repeated in the same small town in California and another small town somewhere else in the country.
(4) A park shelter house is freshly painted in a large city and a small town; the two shelter houses are checked each week for graffiti.
(5) The amount of vandalism at schools in middle-class neighborhoods in a large city and in a small town are compared.

Item 21 is based on the following graph.

CHANGES IN THE PERCENTAGES OF WOMEN IN VARIOUS FIELDS, 1972-1982

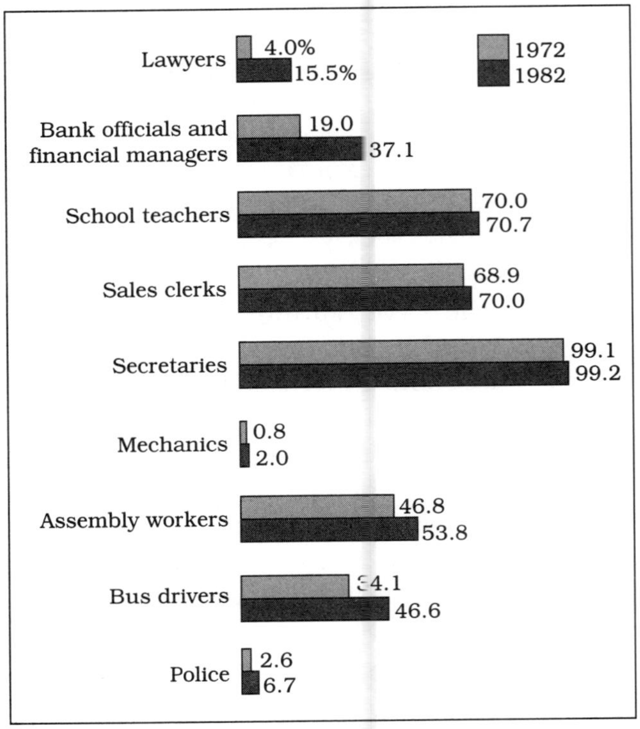

21. Which of the following statements concerning changes over the ten-year period is shown by the figure?

(1) By the end of the period many jobs were fairly evenly divided between male and female workers.

(2) By the end of the period many more men were working in jobs once considered "women's work."

(3) In a number of traditionally male professions the percentage of women workers rose to some extent.

(4) Many women moved from teaching and secretarial work into law and banking.

(5) Many fields once dominated by males came to be dominated by females.

Items 22 and 23 are based on the following information.

In tribal societies, when a person reaches a new stage in life (puberty, marriage, etc.), he goes through an initiation rite. These rites symbolize a change in the individual's status. At the end of the rite, the individual takes on a new role in society, for example, the role of adult as opposed to child.

22. The main purpose of the initiation rites is to

(1) welcome outsiders into a society

(2) signal the beginning of a new phase of life

(3) control the number of people in a society

(4) add excitement to people's lives

(5) mark changes in the seasons

23. In our society there are events that are similar to initiation rites. Such events include all of the following <u>except</u>

(1) an engagement party

(2) a retirement party

(3) a Thanksgiving dinner

(4) a wedding

(5) a graduation ceremony

Items 24 to 27 refer to the following information.

When George M. Pullman built a new factory for producing railroad cars, he decided to build a new town to go with it. This new town, the first planned town in America, was Pullman, Illinois. It was home to the factory's workers.

George Pullman saw his town as a place where workers would not have "to live in crowded and unhealthy tenements, in miserable streets, and subject to all the temptations and snares of a great city." The town Pullman built was both orderly and beautiful.

Pullman also made sure that the town produced money for his company. The company owned the stores and sold the goods people bought. It also owned the houses. Rents were set high enough so the company could make a good profit.

In 1885 an article about the town of Pullman appeared in *Harper's* magazine. The author, Richard Ely, praised the town's beauty, layout, and healthfulness. But he criticized the idea of a "company town": "If free American institutions are to be preserved, we want no [group] reared as underlings.... The idea of Pullman is un-American.... It is benevolent, well-wishing feudalism, which desires the happiness of the people, but in such a way as shall please the authorities."

24. George Pullman built the town of Pullman because

(1) he needed a place where he could produce more railroad cars
(2) he wanted to provide his workers with a healthy environment
(3) he wanted to provide his workers with the cultural stimulation usually found only in big cities
(4) he felt Illinois needed another major urban center
(5) he wanted to correct a serious housing shortage

25. From the passage it's clear that, in building the town, Pullman believed that

(1) good deeds should always be done for their own sake
(2) order and beauty could go hand in hand with making a profit
(3) the idea of the town was un-American.
(4) the company's only goal was to serve its workers
(5) a big city environment would be healthy for workers

26. Ely was critical of the town because he felt that

(1) its reputation for beauty and healthfulness was not deserved
(2) it made the workers too dependent on and subservient to the company
(3) it interfered with the company's making a profit and was therefore "un-American"
(4) it left workers open to all the temptations of a large city
(5) its location was not convenient to the factory and workers had to commute a great distance

27. Which of the following statements is an opinion rather than a fact?

(1) Pullman was America's first planned town.
(2) Factory workers lived in Pullman.
(3) Pullman's company made a profit from rents charged to workers.
(4) Pullman's workers had a better life than factory workers in cities.
(5) Richard Ely's magazine article both praised and criticized Pullman.

Items 28 to 30 refer to the following information.

Desensitization is a method for reducing anxiety. It helps people relax in situations that once caused them anxiety.

The first step in desensitization is to identify the kinds of situations that cause anxiety. People rank situations by the degree of anxiety they cause. The second step is to practice a set of relaxation techniques. The final phase of desensitization is called counterconditioning. People are placed in normally low-anxiety situations. Using the techniques they have learned, they practice relaxing in those situations. Once they learn to relax in low-anxiety situations, they are placed in higher anxiety situations. Again and again the process of learning to use relaxation techniques is practiced.

Desensitization is completed when people remain calm when faced with situations that once caused them high anxiety.

28. Which of the following is the best summary of the passage?

(1) Anxiety can disrupt a person's life.
(2) Some situations cause more anxiety than others.
(3) Some people are more anxious than others.
(4) Desensitization is a process to help people reduce anxiety.
(5) During counterconditioning people are placed in various anxiety-causing situations.

29. On which of the following assumptions is the desensitization method based?

(1) Talking about anxiety is the best way to reduce it.
(2) Anxious people cannot relax and so they must learn to live with their anxieties.
(3) Put to good use, anxiety can be a positive and constructive force in a person's life.
(4) People can learn to change their responses to situations.
(5) People must learn to expect more of themselves.

30. Which of the following might a person who is afraid of flying do during counterconditioning?

(1) make a list of the benefits of flying
(2) talk about childhood experiences that might have caused this fear
(3) listen to a lecture on why airplanes are safer than cars
(4) take an anxiety-reducing medication before going on a plane
(5) sit in a plane on the ground and try to relax

Answers are on page 135–137.

Half-Length Practice Test

Directions: Choose the one best answer for each question.

Items 1 to 5 are based on the following information.

Every society has a set of generally accepted goals and a set of generally accepted rules, or means, for achieving these goals. Individuals may either accept or reject their society's means. Listed below are the five possible patterns of individual behavior in relation to society's goals and means.

(1) conformity — full acceptance of both the goals and the means for achieving them
(2) ritualism — acceptance of the goals and the means but without a clear sense that the purpose of the means is to achieve the goals, so that the individual becomes obsessed with rules and means
(3) retreatism — rejection of the goals but acceptance of the means, so that the individual pursues his or her own objectives while following society's rules
(4) innovation — acceptance of the goals but rejection of the means for achieving them
(5) rebellion — rejection of both the goals and the means

Each of the following describes the behavior of an individual or group in relation to society's goals and means. Assume that the society's primary goal is financial success and that honest hard work is the accepted means for achieving this goal. Choose the behavior pattern that best fits the description. The categories may be used more than once in the set of items. No one question has more than one best answer.

1. A sculptor is interested only in expressing her artistic ideas. She cares nothing about money. Although her sculptures don't bring her much money, she works on them day and night. The behavior pattern described is

(1) conformity
(2) ritualism
(3) retreatism
(4) innovation
(5) rebellion

2. A local politician has achieved great success and is returned to office year after year, thanks largely to an extensive network of "friends" with whom he exchanges favors. He increases his income significantly by taking bribes and kickbacks from city contractors. The behavior pattern described is

(1) conformity
(2) ritualism
(3) retreatism
(4) innovation
(5) rebellion

3. A group of friends live in a commune. Their life revolves around meditation and spiritual growth. They're not interested in money, and the only work they do is to grow enough food to meet their daily needs. The behavior pattern described is

(1) conformity
(2) ritualism
(3) retreatism
(4) innovation
(5) rebellion

4. A well-known surgeon is president of his local medical association. He works hard as both a surgeon and a medical researcher. He lives with his family in an expensive home in the suburbs. His oldest children attend private college. The behavior pattern described is

(1) conformity
(2) ritualism
(3) retreatism
(4) innovation
(5) rebellion

5. A big drug dealer surrounds himself with luxuries. He owns a mansion and a yacht and spends most of his time traveling the world, for both "business" and pleasure. The behavior pattern described is

(1) conformity
(2) ritualism
(3) retreatism
(4) innovation
(5) rebellion

6. One measure of how well or poorly business—and the economy—is doing is the number of incorporations and bankruptcies. Incorporation refers to the formation of a new stockholder-owned company. Bankruptcy refers to the financial failure of a company. In a country whose economy is improving there are

(1) more incorporations and fewer bankruptcies
(2) more bankruptcies and fewer incorporations
(3) more incorporations and more bankruptcies
(4) fewer incorporations and fewer bankruptcies
(5) little change in the numbers of incorporations and bankruptcies

Item 7 refers to the following cartoon.

7. The sign in the cartoon quotes an old nursery rhyme according to which the lack of a nail caused the loss of a battle. The cartoonist makes a comparison in which citizens' failure to vote is the nail. The cartoonist is most likely saying that if American citizens don't vote, then ultimately

(1) they will lose their freedom
(2) their standard of living will drop
(3) America's balance of trade problems will worsen
(4) America will lose its battle against dictatorships abroad
(5) American leadership will be strengthened

Items 8 and 9 refer to the following cartoon.

The big stick in the Caribbean Sea

8. The figure in the cartoon is President Theodore Roosevelt. The cartoon is making a comment on the "Big Stick" policy that Roosevelt developed for the Caribbean area. Which of the following best describes Roosevelt's "Big Stick" policy for the Caribbean?

(1) The United States would stay out of the affairs of these countries.

(2) The United States would give extensive economic aid to these countries.

(3) The United States would trade less with Latin America and more with Europe and Asia.

(4) The United States would act as a sort of policeman in the Caribbean, using force, if necessary, to collect debts and solve other problems.

(5) The United States wanted to hand over leadership of the Western hemisphere to the countries of the Caribbean.

9. The cartoonist uses distortion of size to express an opinion about Roosevelt's "Big Stick" policy. Which of the following statements most accurately characterizes this opinion?

(1) Roosevelt's policy gave too much power to the Caribbean countries.
(2) Roosevelt's Caribbean policy was too weak.
(3) Roosevelt's Caribbean policy left the United States open to military attack.
(4) Roosevelt's Caribbean policy was somewhat exaggerated and excessive.
(5) Roosevelt's Caribbean policy was an appropriate and wise policy.

---

10. Tundra is a treeless arctic area that lies between the northernmost limits of the world's forests and the polar ice cap. Based on this information, which of the following is most likely to be true of tundra regions?

(1) They take up much of the earth's surface.
(2) They are found in all parts of the globe.
(3) They tend to be heavily populated areas.
(4) They are exceptionally rich in minerals.
(5) They cannot support much agriculture.

Item 11 is based on the following graph.

MAJOR OCCUPATION GROUPS OF IMMIGRANTS ADMITTED TO U.S., 1970-1977

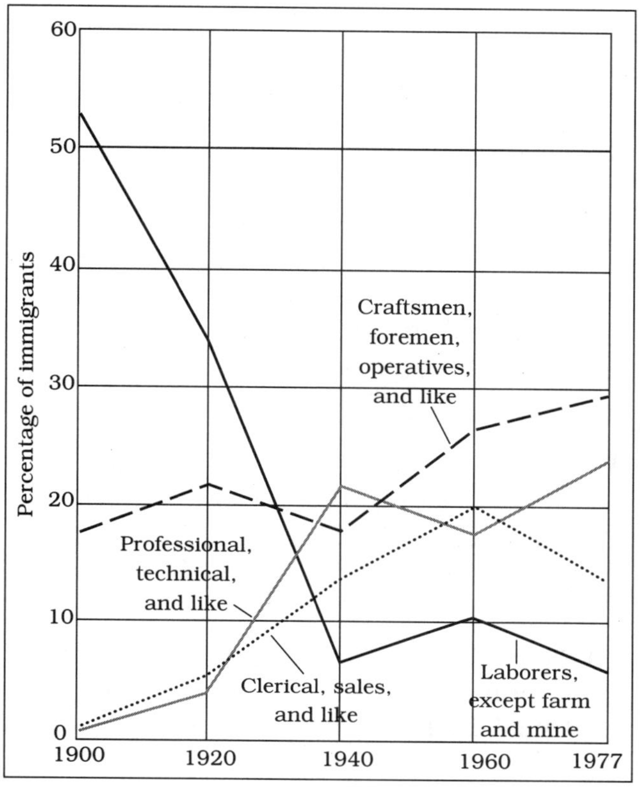

11. From the graph, which of the following conclusions about immigrants admitted to the U.S. can be drawn?

(1) At the turn of the 20th century, most immigrants were skilled workers.
(2) Up until around 1930 most immigrants were not college educated.
(3) In 1940 most immigrants had a trade like carpentry or masonry.
(4) The numbers of immigrants involved in office work has continually risen throughout the period.
(5) Although diverse in their ethnicity, immigrants were similar in their occupations.

Items 12 and 13 are based on the following table.

Distribution of Income:
United States, Mexico, and East Germany
1986

Tenth of Population	United States	Mexico	East Germany
	Percent of National Income		
0–10	1.4	2.0	4.0
10–20	3.4	2.2	6.4
20–30	4.6	2.7	7.5
30–40	5.9	3.3	8.4
40–50	7.1	4.3	9.3
50–60	8.6	5.4	10.3
60–70	10.4	7.2	11.1
70–80	12.8	9.7	12.3
80–90	16.7	14.4	13.8
90–100	29.1	48.8	16.9
	100.0	100.0	100.0

(Poorest ↑ — ↓ Wealthiest)

Source: Leonard Silk, *Economics in Plain English* (rev. ed.) 1986, Simon & Schuster.

0–10 represents the poorest 10th of the population, and 90–100 represents the wealthiest 10th of the population.

12. Which of the following statements is supported by the table?

(1) Distribution of income is essentially similar for the three countries shown.
(2) The poorest in the United States have a greater share of their country's income than the poorest in either Mexico or East Germany.
(3) The wealthiest in the United States have a greater share of their country's income than the wealthiest in Mexico.
(4) Of the three countries, the United States has the most equal distribution of income.
(5) Of the three countries, Mexico has the most unequal distribution of income.

13. Why is it not possible to claim on the basis of the table that the poorest in East Germany are better off than the poorest in the United States?

(1) The poorest in the United States have a larger share of the national income than do the poorest in East Germany.
(2) The table doesn't show how much income each country has.
(3) The table doesn't show what portions of the populations are poorest.
(4) The population of the United States is larger than that of East Germany.
(5) East Germany and the United States are located on different continents.

14. In the years before the Civil War the North's economy was based on manufacturing, while the South's was based on agriculture. Congress, in 1828, passed a tariff on imported manufactured goods. This made the price of these imports much higher than the price of domestic manufactured goods. Many consumers could no longer afford to buy the imports. Most likely, support for the tariff was

(1) strongest from Northern manufacturers
(2) strongest from Southern plantation owners
(3) equal in the North and the South
(4) strong from U.S. consumers but not from U.S. manufacturers
(5) strongest from foreign countries that traded with the United States

Items 15 and 16 are based on the following map.

DAILY SOLAR ENERGY AT THE GROUND, JANUARY
(in calories per square centimeter per day)

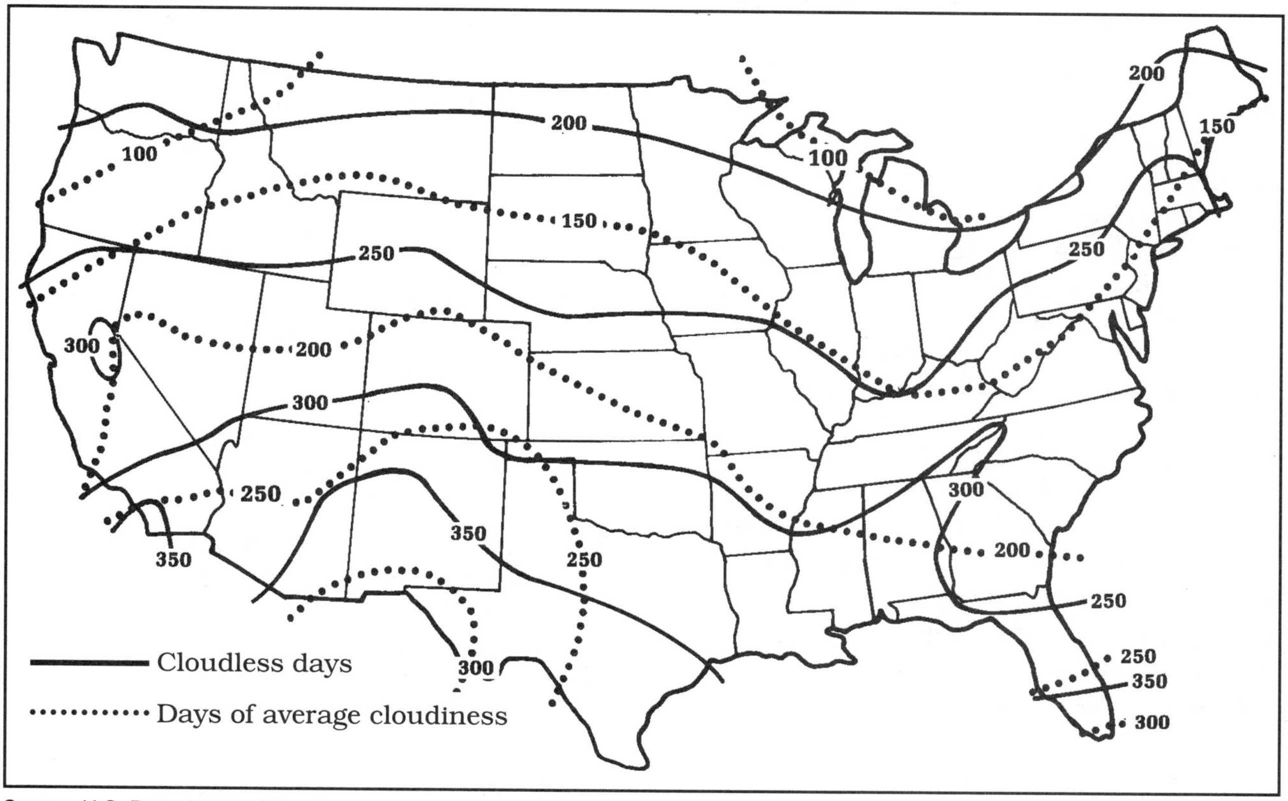

Source: U.S. Department of Energy

15. Which of the following statements is best supported by the map?

(1) Solar energy levels tend to be higher in the southern states than in the northern states.
(2) Solar energy levels tend to be higher on cloudy days than on cloudless days.
(3) Solar energy levels tend to be higher in the summer months than in the winter months.
(4) The United States could meet all its energy needs by using solar energy.
(5) The amount of solar energy received depends largely on elevation.

16. Which of the following regions shows the <u>lowest</u> amount of solar energy reaching the ground on cloudy January days?

(1) the Southwest
(2) the Pacific Northwest
(3) New England
(4) the Plains states
(5) the Southeast

Items 17 to 19 are based on the following information.

Voters are usually given one of two types of ballots on which to mark their choices in an election. Each type of ballot groups candidates differently. On a party column ballot candidates are grouped by party membership. For example, all Republican candidates are listed together. On an office bloc ballot candidates are grouped by the offices they're running for. For example, all candidates for the presidency are listed together

The kind of ballot used affects voting tendencies. The party column ballot encourages voters to vote a straight ticket. That is, it encourages them to cast all their votes for candidates of the same party. The party column ballot therefore helps candidates from a party with an attractive presidential candidate. The office bloc ballot encourages voters to split their tickets. That is, it encourages them to vote for candidates from all parties.

17. Which of the following phrases best summarizes the purpose of the information?

(1) to provide a guide to voting procedures
(2) to describe two kinds of ballots and their effects on voters
(3) to explain the differences between voters and nonvoters
(4) to discuss how ballots are counted
(5) to evaluate the American electoral process

18. A popular President is running for reelection. It is thought that he'll win by a landslide. Other candidates from the President's party are likely to favor a(n)

(1) office bloc ballot, to encourage voters to split their tickets
(2) office bloc ballot, to attract undecided voters
(3) party column ballot, to encourage voters to vote a straight ticket
(4) party column ballot, to encourage more voters to show up at the polls
(5) office bloc ballot, so that candidates will be grouped by the offices they seek

19. Suppose that in an election a state decided to use an office bloc ballot. Which of the following would you expect to happen?

(1) Candidates advertised more on radio than on TV.
(2) Overall voter participation declined.
(3) More older voters participated than younger voters.
(4) The polls accurately predicted who would win the governorship.
(5) Although the governor belonged to one party, most of the state legislators elected were from other parties.

20. When we grow old, our senses become less acute and we tire more easily. Nevertheless, some psychologists have argued that such changes are more than compensated for by the knowledge we've gained from experience. They argue that the productive and creative capacity of older people is often greatly underestimated.

What recommendation would logically follow from the view expressed by these psychologists?

(1) The elderly should be given far better medical care than they currently receive.
(2) Many older people who live on their own should probably be placed in nursing homes.
(3) The income levels of the elderly should be raised by increases in Social Security payments.
(4) The age at which people are forced to retire should be raised.
(5) Older people who are in the work force should be limited to jobs that are easy to do.

Items 21 and 22 are based on the following cartoon.

Source: Eric, *The Atlanta Journal,* with permission

"Come any further and I'll strike!"

21. The person in the cartoon probably

(1) dislikes and fears all machines
(2) is angry because he has a job-related injury
(3) believes that machines are a threat to his job
(4) believes that strikes are ineffective as a weapon of workers
(5) is unaware of the progress made by modern technology

22. Which of the following conclusions is best supported by the cartoon?

(1) Unions are irresponsible.
(2) Humans are too emotional to be reliable workers.
(3) Automation is a threat to society.
(4) Unemployment will decline as a result of automation.
(5) Unemployment will increase as a result of automation.

Item 23 is based on the following information.

One key to strengthening the economy is increased productivity, the hourly output of work...

While American productivity is still increasing, the rate of increase has been even faster in such Pacific Rim countries as Japan, South Korea, and Taiwan, and in some European countries as well. Wages are lower in most other countries, too. As a result, many American products cost more to make than products made in these countries.

(*American Journey*, PH) p. 695

23. All of the following result from U.S. corporations' attempts to make their products more competitive with those of other countries EXCEPT

(1) borrowing Japanese technology
(2) lowering wages in U.S. manufacturing factories
(3) creating new markets in foreign countries to sell U.S. products
(4) manufacturing products in foreign countries where wages are low
(5) using robots and more automated machines in U.S. manufacturing plants

24. The interaction between people and the natural environment is a two-way interaction. People undoubtedly affect their environment but, at the same time, the environment also helps shape human activities.

Which of the following best exemplifies the way the natural environment influences people and their activities?

(1) A warm island nation bases its economy mainly on fishing and the tourist trade.
(2) A large industrial city has very high levels of air pollution.
(3) New methods of irrigation allow a desert to be made into farmland.
(4) The amount of forested area in a country shrinks when trees are cut down and not replaced.
(5) Technological developments affect both the work that people do and their leisure activities.

Items 25 to 28 refer to the following information.

In the late nineteenth century and the early part of this century, many of our cities were in effect run by political "bosses." Bosses were corrupt politicians, who often used the power of their office for their own financial gain. Bosses were able to stay in power by attracting a faithful electorate, which voted them in time after time.

City contracts were a major source of money for the political bosses and their friends. Cities in this era were growing rapidly. There were roads, sidewalks, and docks to be built. There were transportation and sanitation systems to expand. City bosses were in a position to award many profitable contracts. And the companies they awarded contracts to didn't mind kicking some money back to the bosses.

These years were also a time of great immigration. Immigrants and other poor residents of the cities often had problems they needed help with. But this was before the time of public assistance agencies. People didn't know what to do when they lost their jobs or got into trouble. So they often turned to the political bosses. And grateful for the help the bosses gave them, they voted for these bosses each time an election came around.

25. Which of the following best expresses the topic of the passage?

(1) the way bosses were able to abuse power and stay in office
(2) the spread of corruption from city governments to state governments
(3) the contribution immigrants made to America
(4) the growth of industry and of the cities
(5) the procedures for awarding city contracts and how these changed over time

26. Based on the passage, which of the following probably helped end the era of political bosses by depriving bosses of much of their support?

(1) the extension of the vote to women
(2) the creation of national and state welfare programs
(3) greater U.S. involvement in international affairs
(4) the nation's shift from an agricultural economy to an industrial economy
(5) the further growth of cities in the twentieth century

27. Which of the following statements is probably the most accurate characterization of the political system and politics in cities run by bosses?

(1) Democracy no longer existed since citizens weren't allowed to vote.
(2) Democracy existed but in a corrupted form.
(3) Democracy was strengthened.
(4) Elections were marked by lively debate and citizens tended to vote on the basis of issues.
(5) Voters tended to choose new candidates each election.

28. Based on the passage, bosses wanted to stay in power because

(1) immigrants were arriving in large numbers
(2) city politics could often be a steppingstone to a seat in the U.S. Senate
(3) the opportunities for bribes and financial gain were numerous
(4) many people needed their help
(5) a strong hand was needed to make sure the cities grew wisely

Item 29 is based on the following graph.

AVERAGE YEARLY UNEMPLOYMENT RATE, 1890-1990*
(percentage of civilian labor force out of work)

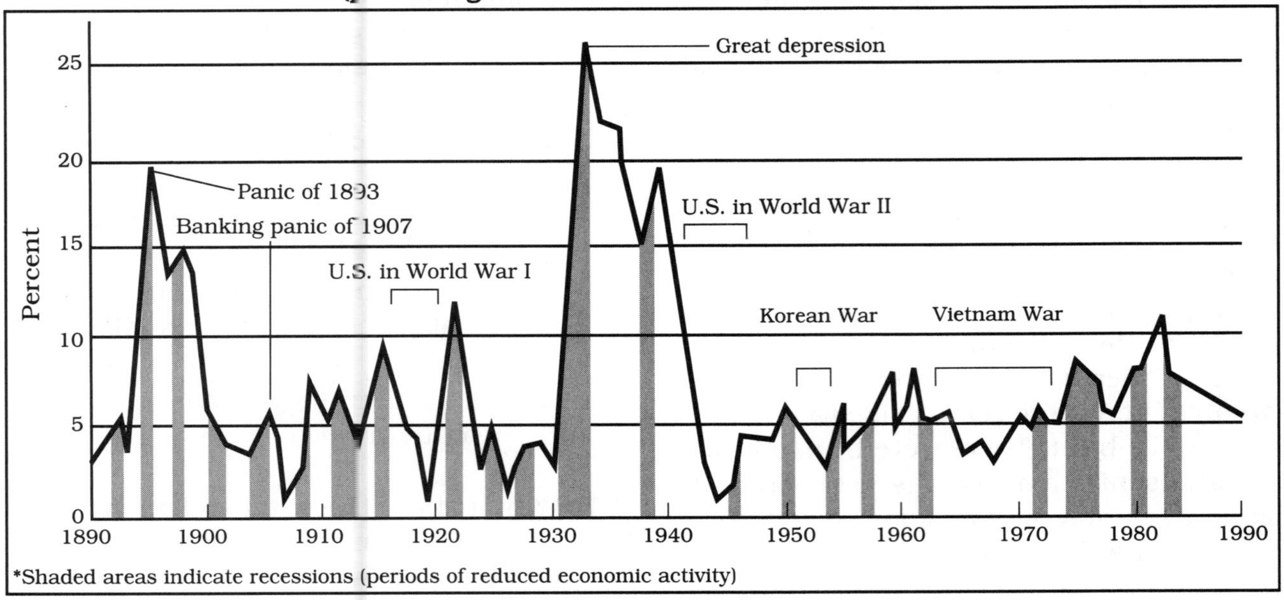

*Shaded areas indicate recessions (periods of reduced economic activity)

Source: U.S. Bureau of Labor Statistics.

29. Which of the following is best supported by the graph?

(1) Wars are associated with high levels of unemployment.

(2) Presidential election years are associated with significant drops in unemployment levels.

(3) Periods of economic difficulty are associated with high levels of unemployment.

(4) The unemployment rate has risen over the past 100 years as machines have eliminated many jobs in the nation's factories.

(5) The unemployment rate in the United States has tended to follow worldwide trends.

30. In order to keep a standard of time, the world has been divided into 24 time zones. Each zone observes a clock time that is one hour earlier than the zone immediately to its east.

Denver, Colorado is two time zones west of Philadelphia, Pennsylvania. If it is 4:00 P.M. in Philadelphia, what time is it in Denver?

(1) 6:00 P.M.

(2) 5:00 P.M.

(3) 4:00 P.M.

(4) 3:00 P.M.

(5) 2:00 P.M.

Items 31 and 32 are based on the following information.

In each chamber of Congress, the majority party gets to choose committee chairpeople. (The majority party is the one with the most Representatives or Senators.) In most cases, the member of the majority party who has been on a committee the longest is chosen as the chairperson. This usually happens even if that Senior member's views don't agree with those of the others from the same party.

31. If the majority of Senators are Republicans and the majority of Representatives are Democrats, most likely the chairperson of the House Agriculture Committee will be

(1) a Democrat just elected to the House for the first time
(2) a Republican with extensive committee experience in the House
(3) the person, from either party, who has served on the House Agriculture Committee the longest
(4) the person on the House Agriculture Committee who received the most votes in the last congressional election
(5) the Democrat with seniority who has served on the House Agriculture Committee

32. You can infer that one advantage of the seniority system is that committee chairpeople

(1) are experienced and familiar with their committees' work
(2) are least likely to increase taxes
(3) represent the views of the rest of their party
(4) bring new ideas and perspectives to the committee
(5) are not influenced by lobbyists

Answers are on pages 138–140.

Half-Length Practice Test

Performance Analysis Chart

Directions: Circle the number of each item that you got correct on the Half-length Practice Test. Count how many items you got correct in each row; count how many items you got correct in each column. Write the amount correct per row and column as the numerator in the fraction in the appropriate "Total Correct" box. (The denominators represent the total number of items in the row or column.) Write the grand total correct over the denominator, **32**, at the lower right corner of the chart. (For example, if you got 28 items correct, write *28* so that the fraction reads *28*/**32.**)

Item Type	History (Chapter 2)	Political Science (Chapter 3)	Economics (Chapter 4)	Geography (Chapter 5)	Behavioral Science (Chapter 6)	TOTAL CORRECT
Comprehension	8, 25	7, 17	21	16		**/6**
Application		18, 19, 31		24, 30	1, 2, 3, 4, 5	**/10**
Analysis	11, 14, 26, 28	32	6, 13, 23	10	20	**/10**
Evaluation	9, 27, 29		12, 22	15		**/6**
TOTAL CORRECT	**/9**	**/6**	**/6**	**/5**	**/6**	**/32**

The chapters named in parentheses indicate where in the *New Revised Cambridge GED Program: Social Studies* you can find specific instruction about each area of Social Studies. You can also find instruction in Unit III Chapter 1 of the *New Revised Cambridge GED Program: Comprehensive Book.*

Full-Length Practice Test

Directions: Choose the one best answer for each question.

Items 1 and 2 are based on the following graph.

IMMIGRATION TO THE UNITED STATES: ANNUAL AVERAGE, 1900-1979

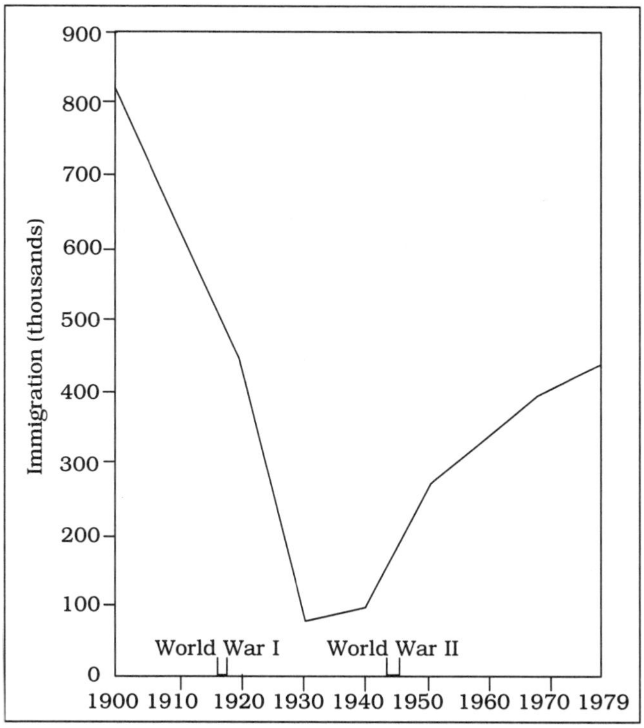

Source: United States Immigration and Naturalization Service

1. Which factor most likely contributed least to the trends shown in the graph?

(1) changes in U.S. immigration laws
(2) the occurrence of wars
(3) changes in economic conditions overseas
(4) changes in economic conditions in the United States
(5) changes in migration patterns within the United States

2. Based on the immigration trends shown, which of the following is least likely?

(1) At the beginning of the century the United States had a highly restrictive immigration policy.
(2) U.S. isolationist attitudes at the end of World War I discouraged immigration.
(3) The Depression of 1929 discouraged immigration.
(4) Following World War II many refugees came to the United States.
(5) In the sixties and seventies an increasing number of people came to the United States to escape conflicts in their home countries.

---

3. A television talk show host has assembled a panel of experts on social issues to answer audience-written questions. Which of the following questions from the audience should the host ask the economist on the panel to answer?

(1) How can more Americans be encouraged to vote?
(2) How can the American educational system be improved?
(3) How can America's trade deficit be lowered?
(4) How can the crime rate be lowered?
(5) How can relations among America's various racial and ethnic groups be improved?

Items 4 to 6 are based on the following information.

Aggression is a very natural response to frustration, according to many psychologists. But aggression can't always be expressed directly. That is, we can't always "target" our aggression at the person who frustrates us. Often, expressing aggression directly at that person would get us into trouble of some sort. As a result, displacement occurs. Displacement means that we act in an aggressive way, but we direct our aggression at someone who seems like a "safer," less threatening target.

4. Which of the following statements is supported by the information?

(1) Displacement can lead to aggression.
(2) Frustration can lead to aggression.
(3) Aggression can lead to frustration.
(4) Aggression can lead to better communication among individuals.
(5) Displacement can lead to severe psychological problems.

5. Which of the following statements is a hypothesis explaining a person's displacement of aggression?

(1) A mother slapped her daughter across the face.
(2) A woman refused to talk to anyone because she was upset.
(3) A man probably yelled at his boss because she docked his pay.
(4) She probably yelled at me instead of her husband because I am her best friend.
(5) Instead of acting aggressively, a woman meditated to displace her frustration.

6. Which of the following best exemplifies displacement?

(1) A salesperson whose customers seem to be backing out of a purchase speaks in a rude and angry way to his secretary.
(2) A person who is having difficulties learning a foreign language feels frustrated.
(3) A person who had a hard day at work decides to go have a good time and forget about work.
(4) An employee whose boss has just yelled at him yells back at the boss.
(5) A consumer who had a bad experience at a particular store decides never to shop there again.

7. Activity space is a term geographers use for the area within which people move in carrying on their usual activities. The typical amount of activity space differs from country to country as well as among individuals.

Which of the following factors likely has the most direct effect on determining the amount of activity space typical in a country?

(1) the language spoken in a country
(2) a country's climate
(3) the amount of natural resources a country has
(4) the extensiveness of a country's transportation system
(5) the stability of a country's economic system

Items 8 and 9 are based on the following maps.

CONTINENTAL DRIFT

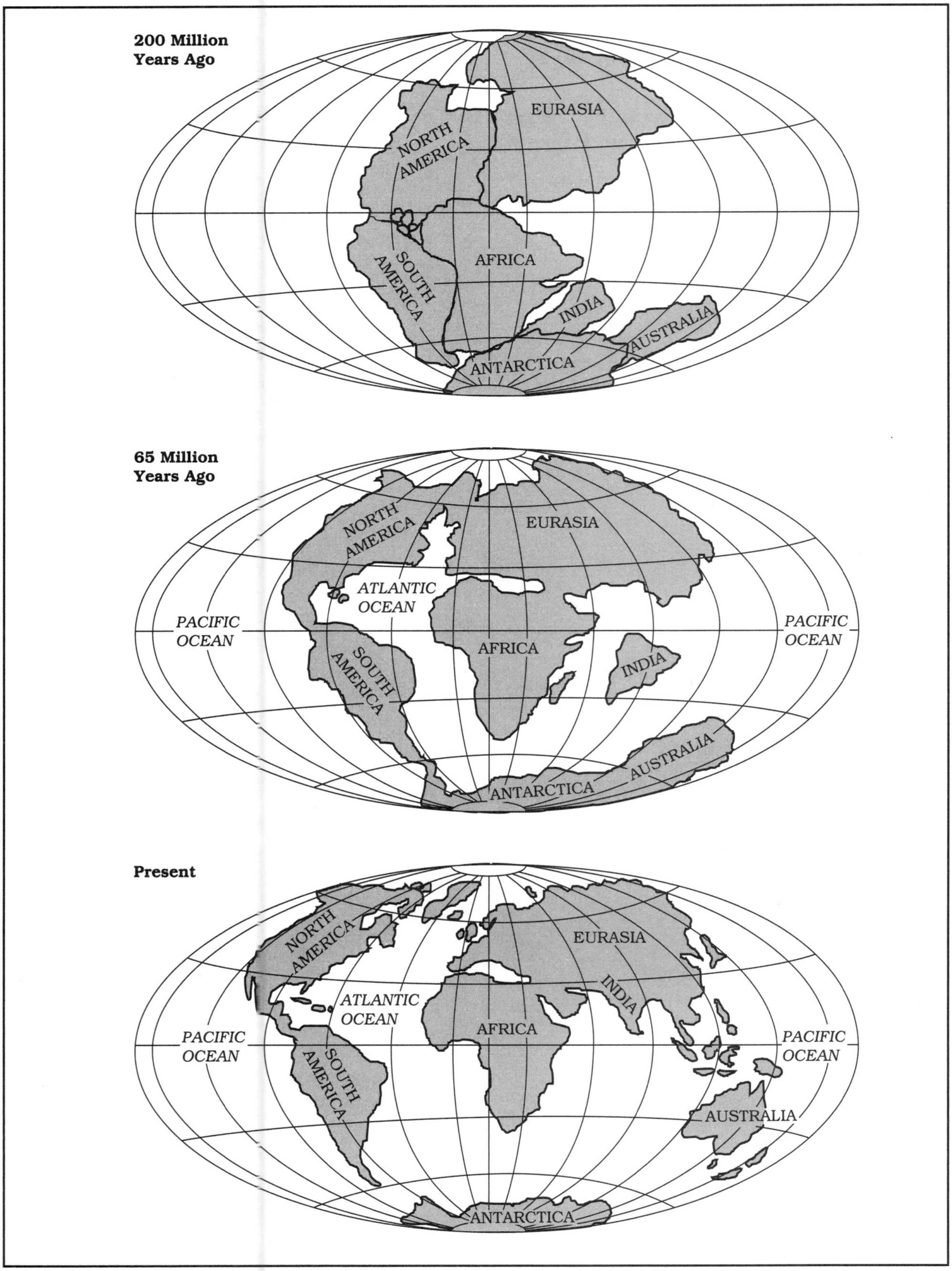

8. Based on the figures, which of the following statements is <u>not</u> true?

(1) Two-hundred million years ago the continents were connected and formed one "supercontinent."
(2) Sixty-five million years ago India had broken away from Antarctica.
(3) Sixty-five million years ago South America had split off from Africa.
(4) Sixty-five million years ago North America had split off from Eurasia.
(5) Australia did not become a separate land mass until some point within the last sixty-five million years.

9. Based on the figures, assuming continental drift continues, which of the following is most likely to be larger sixty-five million years from now?

(1) Africa
(2) Antarctica
(3) the Atlantic Ocean
(4) Australia
(5) the Pacific Ocean

10. Americans use two major types of money: currency and demand deposits. Currency includes paper money and coins. Demand deposits are checks, that is, written orders from the checking account holder to the bank to transfer some of his or her funds to the payee. Most of the money in circulation is not currency. In fact, currency makes up less than one-third of all money.

The largest proportion of money used in the United States is issued by

(1) the United States Treasury
(2) checking account holders
(3) department stores
(4) large corporations
(5) counterfeiters

11. The 1832 South Carolina Ordinance of Nullification said that states had the right to declare laws passed by Congress unconstitutional. Which of the following statements could best be used to support this states' rights position?

(1) Congress is the legitimate representative of the will of the people.
(2) The Supreme Court alone has the power to determine whether laws are constitutional or not.
(3) The Constitution says that when there are conflicts between laws passed by Congress and state laws, the laws passed by Congress are the ones that count.
(4) The federal government was created by the states, and the Constitution reserves many powers for the states.
(5) To become law a bill must be passed by both houses of Congress.

12. The Green Revolution refers to the development of new kinds of wheat and rice, and their use, especially in poorer countries. These new grains produce much higher crop yields than the grains previously used.

The direct effect of the Green Revolution on poorer nations was most likely a(n)

(1) reduction in their dependence on imported manufactured goods
(2) increase in ability to feed their populations
(3) decrease in population growth rates
(4) decrease in exports of agricultural goods
(5) increase in ability to farm desert and mountain areas

Item 13 is based on the following graph.

ECONOMIC EXPECTATIONS OF THE POPULATIONS OF SELECTED COUNTRIES: 1977 AND 1980

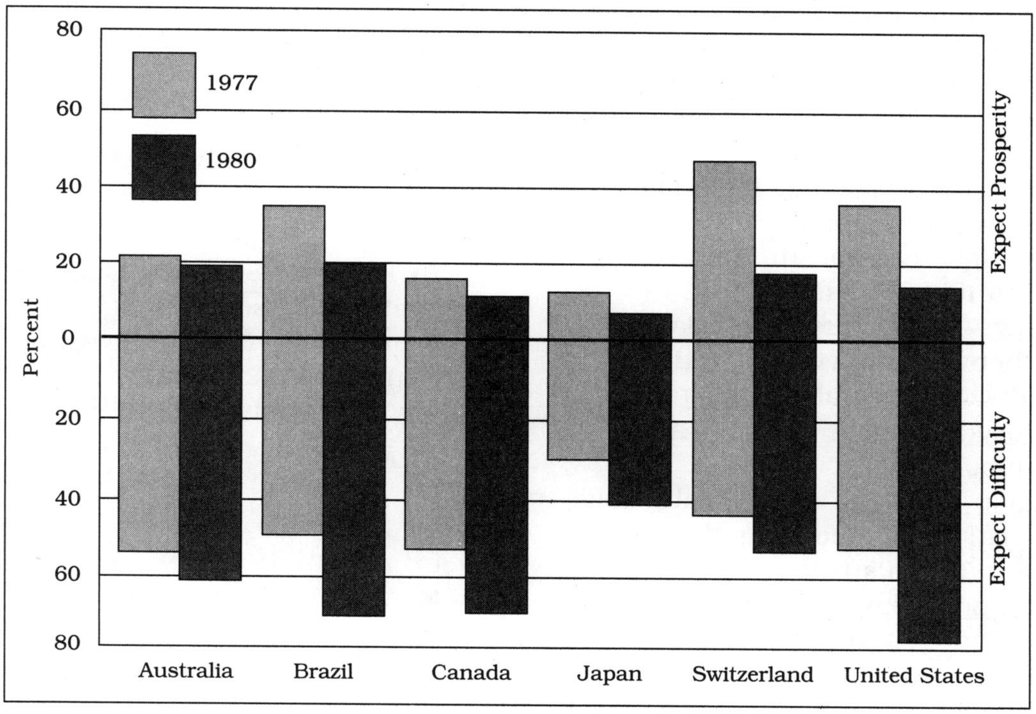

13. The graph indicates that over the three-year period covered

(1) the world economic situation improved significantly
(2) people in most countries became more optimistic about the future
(3) many countries fell into serious economic crises
(4) people in most countries became more pessimistic about the future
(5) the countries of the world became economically more dependent on one another

14. In times when jobs are scarce, workers tend to focus on job security and to be less concerned about other sorts of issues.

Workers are more likely to be interested in job satisfaction in times when

(1) the government plays a greater role in the economy
(2) the economy is doing well
(3) their company is in financial difficulties
(4) unemployment rates are increasing
(5) competition for jobs is increasing

Items 15 to 18 are based on the following information.

Laws are classified by who makes them and what they concern. Listed below are five types of laws used in the American legal system and a brief description of each.

(1) admiralty and maritime law—laws concerning shipping and commerce on the high seas and the waterways of the United States.
(2) civil law—laws concerning relationships between individuals and defining individuals' legal rights
(3) statutory law—laws made by a legislative body
(4) administrative law—laws established by the rules and decisions that government administrators make
(5) constitutional law—laws established by the Constitution and by the Supreme Court's interpretation of the Constitution

Each of the following is an example of one of the types of law described above. Choose the type of law that best fits the example. The types may be used more than once in the set of items. No one question has more than one best answer.

15. A barge that had been carrying goods between states sinks in the Mississippi River. Two companies each claim the right to salvage the cargo. The type of law that is involved is

(1) admiralty and maritime law
(2) civil law
(3) statutory law
(4) administrative law
(5) constitutional law

16. John Jones sues Sam Smith for having falsely accused him of selling shoddy shoes. The type of law that is involved is

(1) admiralty and maritime law
(2) civil law
(3) statutory law
(4) administrative law
(5) constitutional law

17. In 1954 the Supreme Court decided that having separate schools for children of different races violates the Fourteenth Amendment. The type of law that is involved is

(1) admiralty and maritime law
(2) civil law
(3) statutory law
(4) administrative law
(5) constitutional law

18. The Federal Trade Commission, a government regulatory agency, ruled that so-called economy-size packages of a breakfast cereal must have a lower unit price than regular-size packages. The type of law that is involved is

(1) admiralty and maritime law
(2) civil law
(3) statutory law
(4) administrative law
(5) constitutional law

Items 19 to 22 are based on the following information.

In 1959 Fidel Castro overthrew Cuban dictator Fulgencio Batista. Over the following year, Castro's new government moved steadily toward Marxism. He established close relations with the Soviet Union.

When President Kennedy took office in 1961, he learned that the previous administration had authorized the CIA to train Cuban exiles for an invasion to overthrow Castro. The CIA felt that Castro was so unpopular that when the exiles invaded, they would set off a popular uprising against them.

Then the President received a memo from Senator Fulbright, chairman of the Senate Committee on Foreign Relations. Fulbright objected to the plan. Castro did not pose a serious military threat to the United States, he argued. And by helping to overthrow another country's government the United States might hurt its own international reputation.

After listening to the various sides of the issue, President Kennedy decided on a compromise: The invasion would proceed. However, the United States would limit its direct involvement. Plans had called for an American air raid to accompany the mission. Kennedy decided to cancel the air raid.

In April 1961, 1,400 Cuban exiles waded ashore at the Bay of Pigs on the coast of Cuba. However, the expected popular uprising did not occur. The invaders were easily defeated by Castro's forces.

President Kennedy accepted full responsibility for the mission's failure. He also stated he didn't regret having gone through with it. He took the occasion to warn Russia that the United States would "protect this hemisphere against external aggression."

19. Why did President Kennedy order an invasion of Cuba?

(1) He wanted to strengthen U.S. control throughout the Caribbean.
(2) He feared Cuba would become a communist state under Castro.
(3) He wanted to secure the safe return of Cuban exiles living in the U.S.
(4) He knew that Fidel was unpopular.
(5) He was obligated to carry out the invasion plans of the previous Presidential administration.

20. Based on the passage, which of the following provides the best explanation for the failure of the Bay of Pigs invasion?

(1) The Cuban exiles and the CIA underestimated Castro's strength and support.
(2) The Bay of Pigs was a poor location from which to launch an invasion.
(3) The American people wanted the United States to overthrow Castro at any cost.
(4) The exiles were poorly trained.
(5) Delays threw off the timing of the invasion.

21. Which of the following is supported by the passage?

(1) The Russians, in fact, had no contact with Cuba.
(2) Air raids would have guaranteed the success of the mission.
(3) Kennedy wanted to resist Communist penetration of the Western Hemisphere.
(4) The president and Congress lacked all knowledge of CIA activities.
(5) Castro was unpopular in Cuba.

22. Which of the following situations most closely resembles the one described in the passage?

(1) the attempt to rescue American hostages in Iran by helicopter airlift
(2) the use of U.S. marines in the Dominican Republic to collect debts owed to Europeans and Americans
(3) the formation of the brigade of American volunteers to help Spain's left-leaning government in the Spanish Civil War
(4) U.S. support of the Contras, Nicaraguan rebels attempting to oust the Marxist Sandinista government in their country
(5) President Wilson's dispatch of U.S. troops to cross the Mexican border and capture bandit Pancho Villa

Items 23 and 24 are based on the following table.

Men's and Women's Earnings by Income Bracket
(percentage of full-time workers in each income group)

	Men	**Women**
Less than $5,000	2.9	3.3
$5,000–$10,000	6.6	15.6
$10,000–$15,000	12.8	27.5
$15,000–$20,000	14.6	21.6
$20,000–$25,000	14.3	14.9
$25,000–$35,000	23.4	12.0
$35,000–$50,000	15.4	3.5
More than $50,000	9.1	1.0

23. Which of the following facts explains why the percentage of men earning $25,000–$35,000 is almost double that of women?

(1) Men work harder than women.
(2) Women have been discriminated in the workplace.
(3) Men are more ambitious in pursuing higher paying jobs.
(4) Many women are forced to stay home to care for young children.
(5) Men like to work more overtime than women.

24. Which of the following patterns emerge from the comparison of men's and women's earnings?

(1) There are fewer women in the labor force than there are men.
(2) The women's movement helped bring about significant increases in women's wages.
(3) Many mothers of young children work on only a part-time basis.
(4) Equal numbers of men and women are now enrolled in institutions of higher education.
(5) There are more women than men in traditionally low-paying jobs.

---

25. Which of the following research topics related to crime would most interest a psychologist?

(1) How rapidly has the crime rate risen in twentieth-century America?
(2) What kinds of crime are most common in the United States today?
(3) How do attitudes toward crime differ from culture to culture?
(4) Are there any personality factors that make individuals more likely or less likely to commit crimes?
(5) Do urban environments have higher crime rates than rural environments?

26. A trade deficit occurs when a country spends more money on imports than it earns from exports. To reduce the deficit, a policy should

(1) prevent unsafe products from being imported
(2) limit the quantity of imports
(3) counteract environmental dangers created by imports
(4) make sure imports don't threaten U.S. national security
(5) encourage Americans to buy more imported goods

Item 27 is based on the following cartoon.

MacNelly, *Chicago Tribune*. Reprinted by permission of Tribune Media Services.

27. Which statement best expresses the message of the cartoon?

(1) Tax reform wasn't necessary.
(2) The new tax code has not necessarily made the tax laws simpler.
(3) The new tax code has meant less work for taxpayers and tax accountants.
(4) The old tax code was favored by taxpayers and tax accountants.
(5) The Internal Revenue Service should publish additional tax code books every year.

---

28. North Americans' high standard of living has been made possible by rapid economic growth. This economic growth, in turn, has been made possible by the availability of energy resources. So far we have relied mainly on fossil fuels such as coal and oil to provide energy. But these are nonrenewable resources. That is, coal and oil exist in only limited quantities, and when they are used up they can't be replaced.

The information suggests that in order to maintain and improve our standard of living, we will have to

(1) increase the average human life span
(2) slow economic growth
(3) use more coal and oil
(4) depend more on sources of energy other than fossil fuels
(5) lower the cost of coal and oil

29. Consumer demands and product price are directly related: The price of a product tends to be higher when consumer demand for that product is high. Prices tend to fall when demand is low.

Which of the following best exemplifies how a consumer could take advantage of the relationship between price and demand?

(1) buying an air conditioner in September
(2) repairing an old television set rather than buying a new one
(3) paying for a new car with cash rather than by getting a loan
(4) shopping around for the best price before buying a new refrigerator
(5) buying a bathing suit in June

Items 30 to 33 are based on the following information.

As the United States expanded westward, the issue of slavery arose repeatedly. Congressmen from Southern and Northern states hotly debated the issue, often reaching compromises that satisfied neither side. The following are some laws that Congress passed.

<u>Northwest Ordinance of 1787</u>—Slavery was banned in the territories that later become Ohio, Indiana, Michigan, Illinois, and Wisconsin.
<u>Compromise of 1820</u>—Maine could enter the Union as a free state and Missouri could enter as a slave state. The territory of the Louisiana Purchase north of the 36°30' parallel was closed to slavery.
<u>Compromise of 1850</u>—California could enter the Union as a free state. Those people living in the rest of the territory acquired from Mexico would decide for themselves whether or not they wanted to establish slavery
<u>Kansas-Nebraska Act of 1854</u>—The Compromise of 1820 was partially repealed. The territory of the Louisiana Purchase was no longer definitively closed to slavery. Instead, the inhabitants would decide for themselves whether or not they wanted to adopt slavery.

30. You can conclude that the purpose of the four laws described above was to

(1) end slavery in the United States
(2) establish how large a state's population should be before admission to the Union
(3) improve the conditions of slaves in the new states and territories
(4) settle whether there should be slavery in new states and territories
(5) decide whether to purchase or otherwise acquire new territory

31. Two of the acts are called compromises (the Compromise of 1820 and the Compromise of 1850). According to the passage, who were these compromises most likely between?

(1) slaves and slaveowners
(2) Americans and Mexicans
(3) members of Congress who argued for territorial expansion and members who opposed it
(4) Northern free states and Southern slave states
(5) Eastern states and Western states

32. Popular sovereignty is a term that means "people's will" and refers to the ability of citizens to decide issues for themselves. Which two of the acts allowed at least some popular sovereignty?

(1) the Northwest Ordinance and the Compromise of 1820
(2) the Northwest Ordinance and the Compromise of 1850
(3) the Kansas–Nebraska Act and the Compromise of 1850
(4) the Compromise of 1820 and the Compromise of 1850
(5) the Kansas–Nebraska Act and the Compromise of 1820

33. The passage best supports the conclusion that Congress

(1) was not interested in the issue of slavery in the territories
(2) refused to pass laws on the issue of slavery in the territories because the issue seemed too explosive
(3) always allowed people within territories to decide for themselves whether or not to accept slavery
(4) always reserved for itself the right to decide whether territories should be open or closed to slavery
(5) did not follow a consistent policy on the issue of whether to allow slavery in new territories and states

Items 34 to 37 are based on the following diagram.

THE ROUTE OF A BILL THROUGH CONGRESS

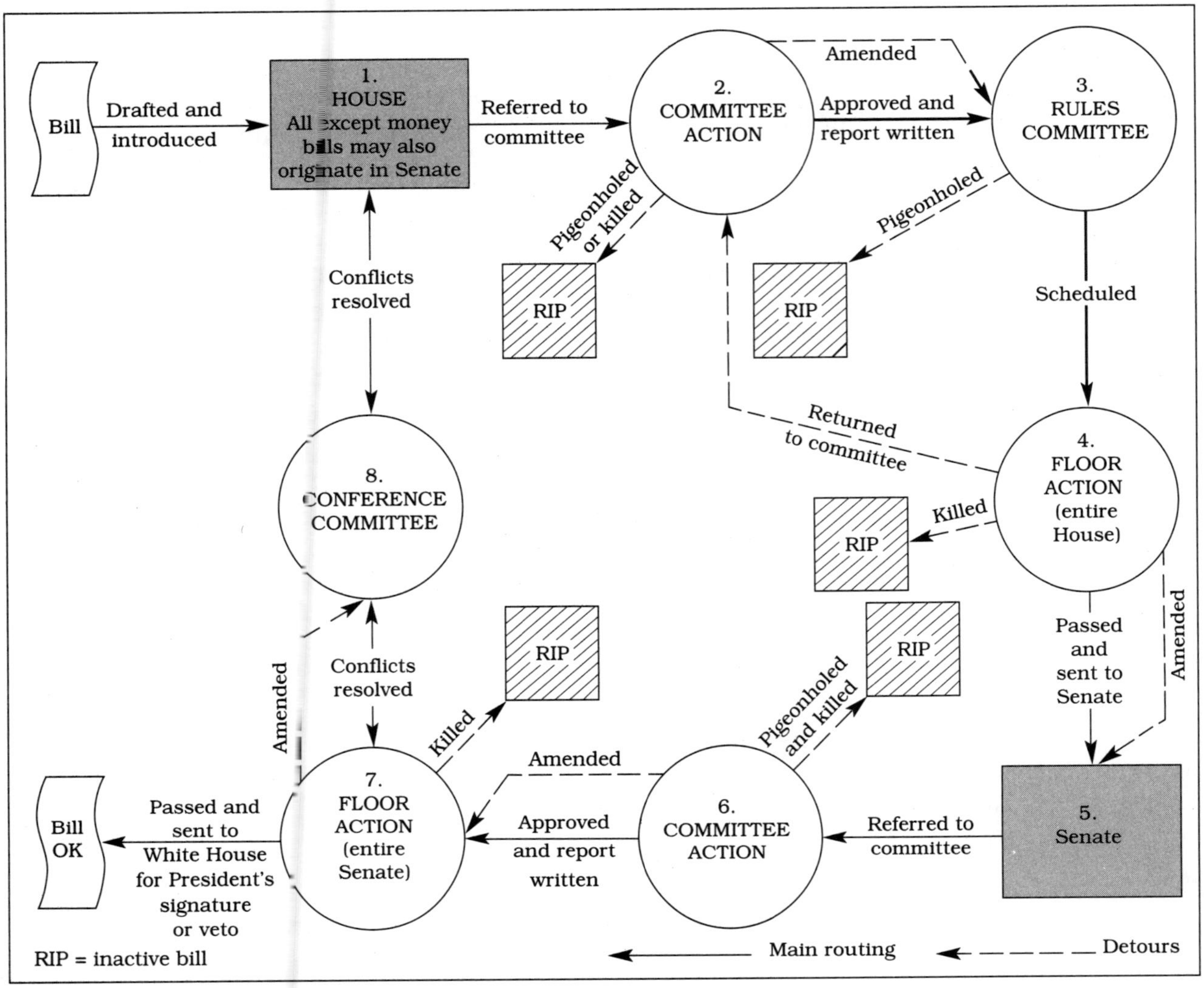

34. The main purpose of this diagram is to show that

(1) the House has a Rules Committee

(2) most bills can be introduced in either the House or the Senate

(3) bills go through many stages before they can become laws

(4) the president may sign or veto bills

(5) the Supreme Court may decide that an act of Congress is unconstitutional

35. Which of the following ideas probably underlies the system for passing bills?

(1) Any bill that is introduced into Congress deserves to be passed.

(2) Bills should be acted on with maximum speed.

(3) Bills should be carefully considered and any problems ironed out before they become laws.

(4) Once a bill has been looked at by the appropriate committees, there's no need for the entire House or Senate to consider it.

(5) Congress should just write rough drafts of bills and let the president work out the details.

36. Which of the following statements is not true?

(1) Bills can be amended or killed by House or Senate committees.

(2) Once bills have left a committee they cannot be returned to that committee.

(3) The House has a Rules Committee, which schedules bills, but the Senate does not.

(4) Bills concerning the budget must originate in the House.

(5) Not all bills that are introduced in the House make it to the Senate.

37. Based on the figure, the purpose of the conference committee is to

(1) decide whether a particular bill should originate in the House or the Senate

(2) settle problems between House and Senate versions of bills

(3) give the House and the Senate a chance to reexamine bills they'd earlier killed

(4) give the public a chance to debate bills that Congress has passed

(5) give the president a chance to see bills that Congress has passed

---

38. Porkbarrel legislation refers to bills that seek to fund unnecessary but popular projects. When congresspeople support such legislation, they probably hope to

(1) improve their chances of reelection

(2) reduce government spending

(3) provide much-needed low-cost housing

(4) make tax cuts possible

(5) improve the nation's transportation system

Item 39 refers to the following cartoon.

—Copyright ©1986 by Herblock in *The Washington Post*

"It's more than we've put out before"

39. The cartoon is a commentary on President Lyndon Johnson's "War on Poverty" programs to help the urban poor. (The figure holding the rope is President Johnson.) Which of the following summarizes the cartoonist's opinion on the War on Poverty programs?

(1) They were the latest in a long line of successful government programs to help the poor.

(2) They would be adequate, even though government programs in the past hadn't done enough to help the poor.

(3) They wouldn't solve the nation's urban and poverty problems.

(4) They had already met the needs of the urban poor.

(5) They were wasting money that would be better spent on military defense.

Items 40 to 44 are based on the following information.

Cultural geography, one of the two main branches of geography, can be subdivided into several smaller areas. Listed below are five areas of cultural geography, with a brief description of each.

(1) Historical cultural geography—the study of how human cultures have evolved in relation to the environment
(2) Population geography—the study of the growth and distribution of human groups in relation to the environment
(3) Natural resources geography—the study of humans' use of the materials provided by their environment
(4) Political geography—the study of the earth's division into nations and other human-made administrative units
(5) Urban geography—the study of how cities have grown and developed in relation to the environment

In each of the following items there is an example of something that would be studied by cultural geography. Choose the area of cultural geography that each example best fits. An area may be used more than once in the set of items, but no item has more than one best answer.

40. St. Petersburg (formerly Leningrad) was founded in 1703 to give Russia an outlet to the Baltic Sea. And because of its location on the Baltic Sea, the city of St. Petersburg grew rapidly. This example best fits

(1) historical cultural geography
(2) population geography
(3) natural resources geography
(4) political geography
(5) urban geography

41. People employ solar or the sun's energy to heat their homes and offices. Unfortunately, solar energy is often least available in climates where it is most needed. This example best fits

(1) historical cultural geography
(2) population geography
(3) natural resources geography
(4) political geography
(5) urban geography

42. The polar regions, although large, have unfavorable climate conditions. They therefore do not have many inhabitants. This example best fits

(1) historical cultural geography
(2) population geography
(3) natural resources geography
(4) political geography
(5) urban geography

43. Early peoples hunted and gathered food. But eventually their environments could no longer easily support them. Therefore people gradually shifted from hunting and gathering to agriculture. The shift to agriculture led to many changes in the way people lived. This example best fits

(1) historical cultural geography
(2) population geography
(3) natural resources geography
(4) political geography
(5) urban geography

44. The present boundaries of many nations in Africa, Asia, and the Americas are the result of arbitrary decisions of the Europeans who colonized these areas. Often these divisions between countries have little to do with earlier tribal boundaries. This example best fits

(1) historical cultural geography
(2) population geography
(3) natural resources geography
(4) political geography
(5) urban geography

---

45. Television networks make projections about election results. That is, they pick a winner as soon as some of the earliest ballots have been counted. Networks have been asked not to broadcast projections for presidential elections until polls on the West Coast have closed. The fear is that earlier broadcasts could affect voter turnout on the West Coast.

Why have networks been asked to delay projecting presidential election results?

(1) Such projections are usually not accurate.
(2) Early projections could make West Coast voters who haven't yet gone to the polls feel that their votes wouldn't count and, thus, not vote.
(3) Voters on the West Coast would find projected results boring.
(4) Television networks would have time to focus more attention on congressional elections.
(5) West Coast voters could be influenced to choose the same candidate selected by East Coast voters.

46. In the 1860s the government of France under Napoleon III sent an army to Mexico and proclaimed a Frenchman Emperor of Mexico. Protesting this action, the United States sent an army of its own to Mexico. On which of the following policy approaches was U.S. action most likely based?

(1) isolationism, in which the United States attempted to avoid all involvement in foreign affairs
(2) the Monroe Doctrine, in which the United States stated that European countries must not interfere in the countries of North and South America
(3) The Open Door policy which said that all countries should have equal trading rights
(4) neutrality, in which the United States refused to take sides in disputes between other countries
(5) détente, in which the United States tried to ease tensions with countries with which it had strained relations

Item 47 is based on the following paragraph.

Businesses have two different kinds of costs. Fixed, or overhead, costs are those costs that do not really vary or change with amount of output. Variable, or direct, costs, in contrast, are directly related to production and change as the firm produces more or less. If all fixed and variable costs are added together, total cost is obtained.

47. According to the paragraph, which of the following is a variable cost?

(1) rent on a building
(2) labor costs
(3) property taxes
(4) interest payments on an outstanding loan
(5) monthly payment for the new computer system

Item 48 is based on the following paragraph.

One very interesting phenomenon in human learning is the formation of *phobias.* Phobias are irrational fears of particular things, activities, or situations. People have had their lives disrupted by fears of high places (acrophobia), closed places (claustrophobia), cats, spiders, snakes, and busy public places (agoraphobia), among others. Many of us are fearful of a visit to the dentist or of making a speech, but in some people these situations can provoke a major panic attack in which the sufferer is unable to catch his or her breath, sweats profusely or shakes from an uncontrollable chill, and even has convulsions and passes out.

(*Psychology,* PH, p. 182)

48. Which of the following situations could bring on a panic attack in a phobic person?

(1) dining in a large, uncrowded restaurant
(2) smoking a cigarette in a smokers' lounge
(3) cleaning the cage of one's pet snake
(4) riding on a public bus at 6:00 A.M., Sunday
(5) flying from Boston to New Orleans on a jet

49. After Andrew Jackson won the Presidential election of the United States, he filled 20 percent of the federal posts with loyal party members. A Jackson supporter attempted to justify those appointments with which of the following statements?

(1) "The race is not to the swift."
(2) "To the victor belong the spoils."
(3) "With malice toward none and charity toward all, we will strive to bind up the nation's wounds."
(4) "May the best man win."
(5) "Ask not what your country can do for you—ask what you can do for your country."

Item 50 is based on the following map.

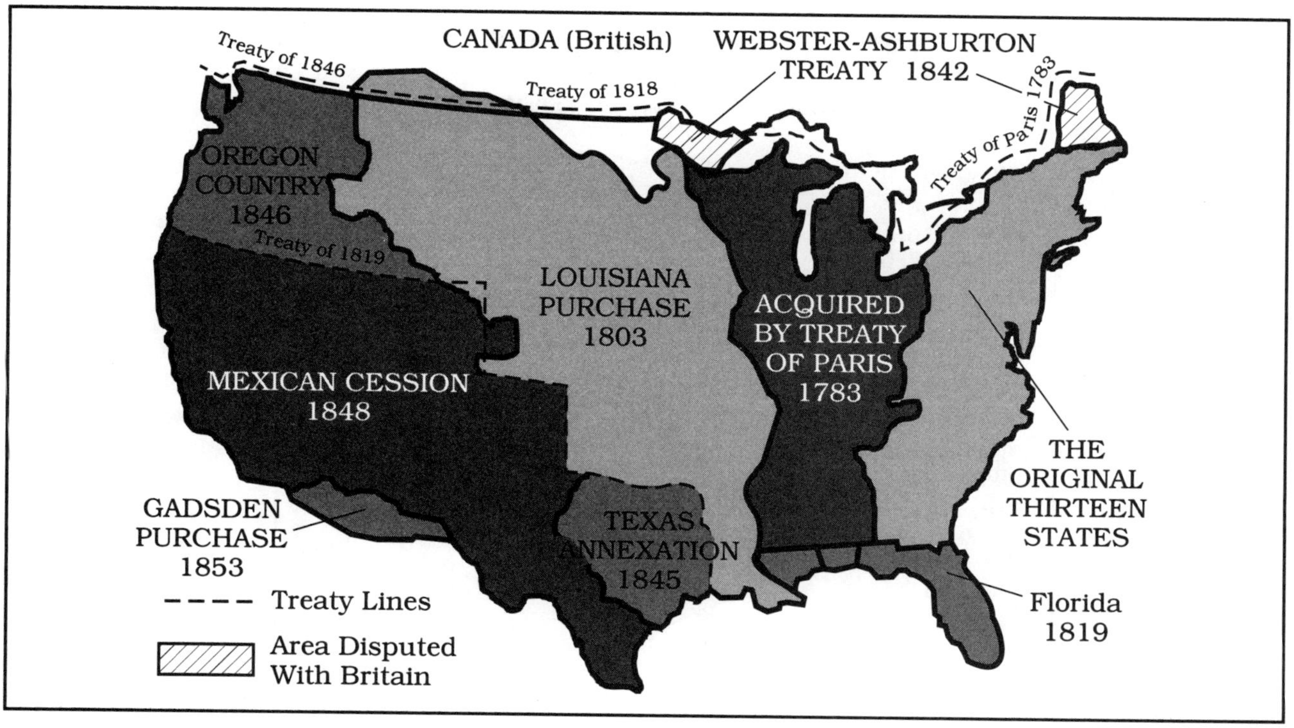

50. According to the map, which of the following statements is not true?

(1) The expansion of the United States proceeded in a strictly east-to-west direction.

(2) The United States acquired territory by several different means and from several different nations.

(3) The area that is now the state of Maine was once disputed with Britain.

(4) The Louisiana Purchase almost doubled the size of the United States.

(5) The Gadsden Purchase completed the continental United States.

51. Logrolling is a practice by which members of Congress agree to vote automatically for each other's pet projects. They apply the principle: "If you scratch my back, I'll scratch yours."

Which of the following is most likely to be a consequence of this practice?

(1) Projects are sometimes approved without being examined as carefully as they should be.

(2) The presidential veto is rarely used.

(3) The president's role in the legislative process is increased.

(4) The process of passing a bill is greatly lengthened.

(5) Congress focuses its attention on cutting the budget deficit.

Items 52 and 53 are based on the following graph.

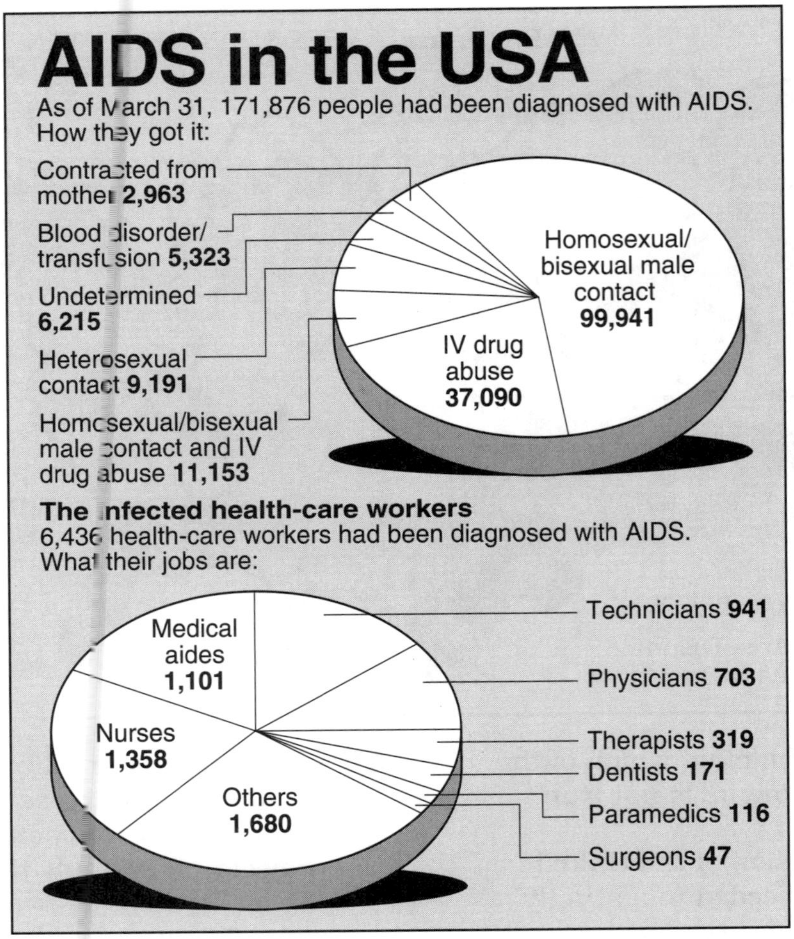

Source: Centers for Disease Control, *USA Today* 5-17-91, p.2A

52. Considering that AIDS is a disease that is spread through the exchange of bodily fluids such as blood and semen, which of the following conclusions concerning the people included in this graph would be incorrect?

(1) The heterosexuals used lamb skin condoms.

(2) The homosexuals did not use any type of condom.

(3) Many of the drug abusers participated in needle-exchange programs to get sterilized needles.

(4) The mothers of children with AIDS were infected with the virus also.

(5) The blood used in transfusions was contaminated with the AIDS virus.

53. Which of the following is the most likely explanation for the large numbers of medical aides and nurses diagnosed with AIDS compared to the low numbers of surgeons, paramedics, and dentists?

(1) Nurses and aides do not use rubber gloves with patients.

(2) Nurses and aides deal directly with patients' blood.

(3) Surgeons, paramedics, and dentists are better informed about protective measures.

(4) Nurses and aides are involved in more emergency procedures with little time to take precautions.

(5) Nurses and aides have more frequent, day to day contact with patients for longer periods of time.

54. People who are elected to office because they are members of a popular, current President's party—not because they, themselves, are popular—win because of the coattail effect.

Which of the following candidates likely benefits most from the coattail effect?

(1) a popular candidate whose party is out of the White House
(2) a popular candidate who belongs to the same party as the currently unpopular president
(3) a little-known candidate who belongs to the same party as a popular president
(4) a little-known candidate whose party is out of the White House
(5) a little-known candidate who belongs to the same party as the currently unpopular president

Items 55 to 58 are based on the following information.

Gross National Product (GNP) is used to measure how a country's economy is doing. GNP is the total dollar value of all goods and services produced in a country in a given year. Therefore, a high GNP means that many goods and services are being produced and the country's economy is doing well.

GNP is an important tool for economists. But economists know it is also a very rough tool. Because it can present a misleading picture, to make the picture clearer, economists have developed two other measures of economic health based on GNP.

GNP doesn't take into account the effects of inflation. Inflation pushes prices up. Thus, when inflation is high, GNP—the total dollar value of goods and services produced—will rise even if no more goods and services are being produced than had been produced before. Economists have therefore developed another measure, called "real GNP." Real GNP is the total value of goods and service once the effects of inflation have been eliminated.

GNP also doesn't take into account the effects of population growth. Assume that a country has a high birth rate. Its population increases very rapidly. Assume also that the GNP is rising. Since GNP is rising, the country is wealthier. But, because of the population growth, this increased wealth must be shared among many more people. Although the nation overall is wealthier, its individuals may be poorer. To take the effect of population size into account, economists have developed a measure called "per capita GNP." Per capita GNP is obtained by dividing GNP by the total number of people in a country. It means gross national product per person.

55. The three economic tools discussed in the passage (GNP, real GNP, and per capita GNP) in some way measure or take into account all of the following <u>except</u>

(1) how well a country's economy is doing
(2) the total value of goods and services produced
(3) inflation
(4) population size and growth
(5) the rate at which a country taxes its citizens

56. In a recent year, the People's Republic of China had a GNP of $121.8 billion and Sweden had a GNP of $32.5 billion. Yet Sweden is wealthier than China, and its citizens have a higher standard of living. Which of the following statements most likely explains this seeming contradiction?

(1) A high GNP means that a country's economy is doing well.
(2) Since the rate of inflation in the two countries may have been different, real GNP figures would be needed for an accurate comparison.
(3) Since the population of Sweden and China are very different in size, per capita GNP figures would be needed for an accurate comparison.
(4) China is more dependent on imports than Sweden is.
(5) China and Sweden use currencies with different values.

57. Real GNP will be lower than GNP when

(1) inflation is high
(2) there is no inflation
(3) population growth is high
(4) population growth is low
(5) inflation and population growth are both zero

58. Assume that it is a Presidential election year. Economists say that the GNP has grown and that inflation has also been high. The president, who's running for reelection, wants to take credit for favorable developments during his first term. The challenger, in contrast, wants to point out problems. Which of the following will the president and the challenger do?

(1) The president will focus on the GNP, the challenger on real GNP.
(2) The challenger will focus on GNP, the president on real GNP.
(3) The president will focus on GNP, the challenger on per capita GNP.
(4) The president will focus on the economy, the challenger will avoid all economic issues.
(5) The challenger will focus on the economy, the president will avoid all economic issues.

59. In recent years the birth rate among women over 30 has risen. This trend is especially evident among professional women. Many of the babies being born to women in this group are first children. These women seem to place a high value on which of the following?

(1) careers
(2) privacy
(3) life experience
(4) education
(5) travel

60. The United States' bicameral, or two-chamber, legislature is part of its checks and balances system. Bills must be approved by both the House and the Senate. They therefore receive more careful consideration than if they passed only one chamber's scrutiny.

An advantage of having a bicameral system instead of a unicameral (one-chamber) system is that it

(1) speeds up the process of considering bills
(2) allows the president to veto bills
(3) provides for a more thorough review of bills
(4) makes the legislature more powerful than the president
(5) encourages qualified individuals to serve in the legislature

Items 61 and 62 are based on the following information.

In our society the traditional sex-role attitudes are that men should support the family and women should take care of the home. Researchers conducted a study to see whether couples in different life situations had these traditional sex-role attitudes or had more nontraditional sex-role attitudes. The four life situations looked at were: (1) not yet married, (2) married but with no children, (3) married and expecting first child, and (4) recent parents. The results are shown in the figure.

SEX-ROLE ATTITUDES IN DIFFERENT LIFE SITUATIONS

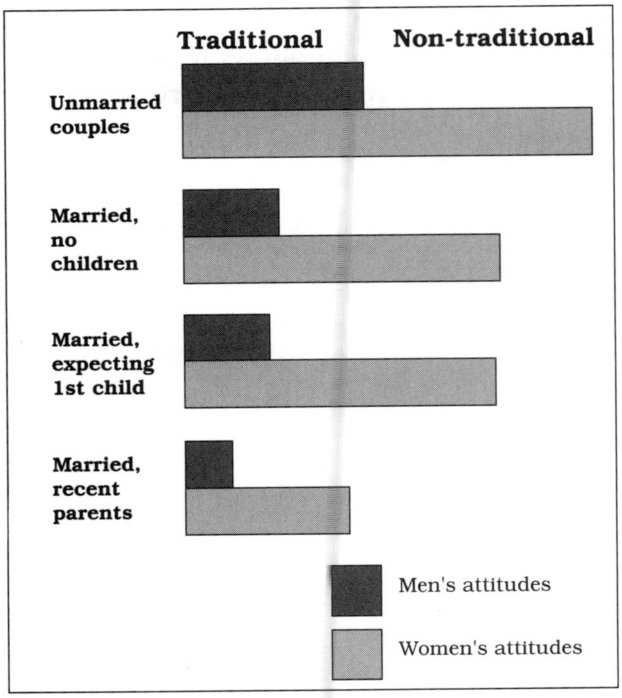

61. Which of the following people is most likely to have most <u>nontraditional</u> sex-role attitudes?

(1) a single man
(2) a single woman
(3) a married woman who doesn't have children
(4) a woman who has recently become a parent
(5) a man who has recently become a parent

62. Which of the following conclusions about sex-role attitudes is best supported by the figure?

(1) People's sex-role attitudes never change.
(2) Men's sex-role attitudes change but women's never do.
(3) Sex-role attitudes are more traditional in some parts of the country than in others.
(4) Men whose parents had nontraditional sex-role attitudes also have nontraditional sex-role attitudes.
(5) Men tend to have more traditional sex-role attitudes than women do.

Item 63 is based on the following map.

UNITED STATES WATER POWER RESOURCES

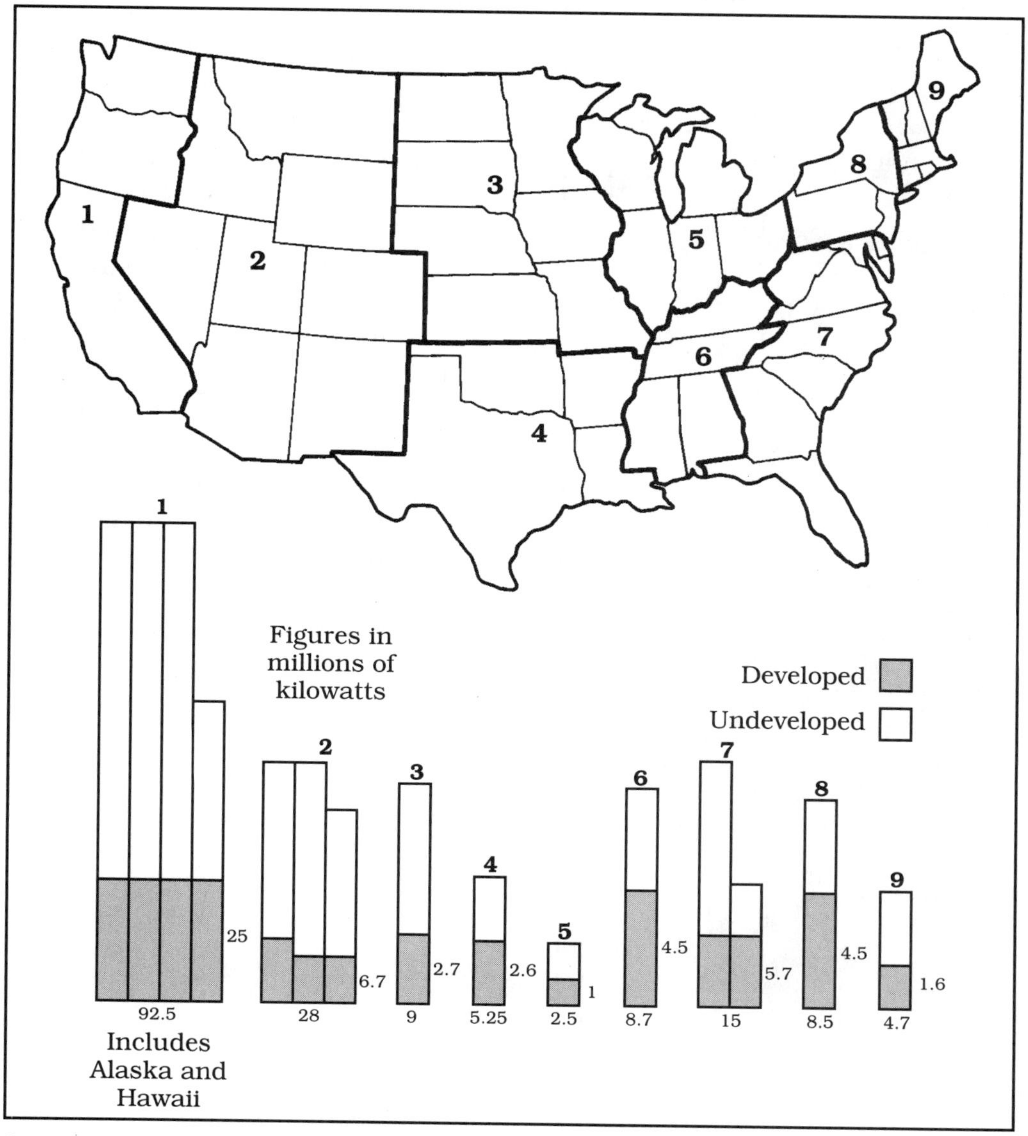

Source: Federal Power Commission

63. Waterpower is of significant importance to industry. Which of the following statements about waterpower in the United States is supported by the map?

(1) Waterpower resources are distributed fairly evenly throughout the United States.

(2) The Northeastern and New England states have already developed nearly all their waterpower resources.

(3) The Midwestern states have not developed any of their waterpower resources.

(4) The greatest potentials for waterpower development are in the Mountain and Pacific States.

(5) If most of the undeveloped waterpower in America is developed, the nation will no longer need to rely on imported oil.

Item 64 is based on the following maps.

NORTH AMERICA IN 1689

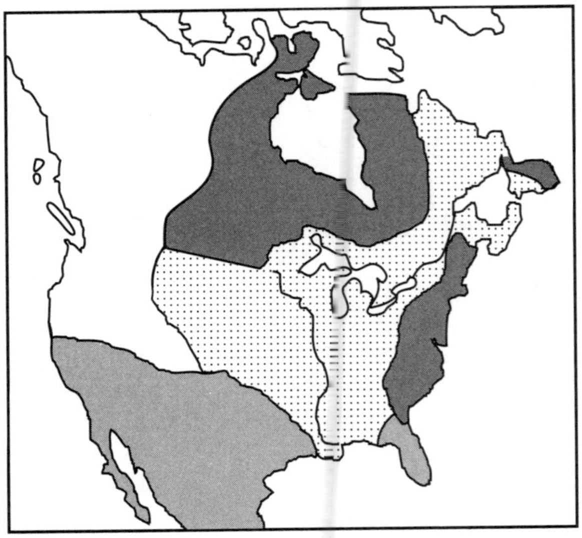

NORTH AMERICA IN 1763

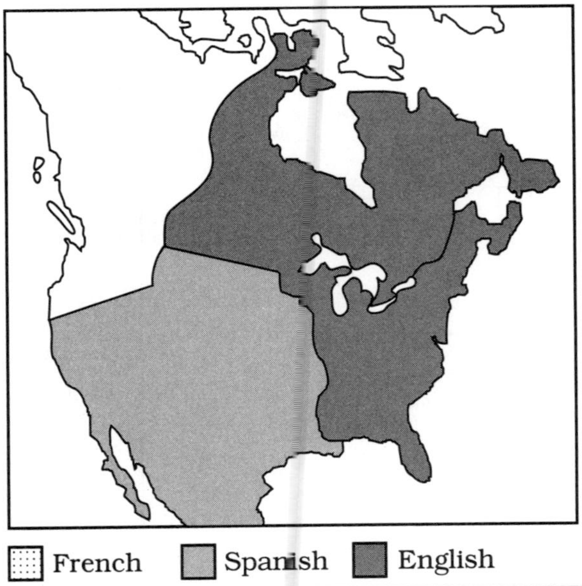

64. On the basis of the maps it can be determined that between 1689 and 1763

(1) Spain expanded its colonial empire in both North America and South America
(2) France was eliminated as a colonial power in North America
(3) Britain had expanded its colonial empire but was losing its grip over part of it due to discontent in the North American colonies
(4) fighting often broke out between the British and Spanish in North America
(5) Britain decided to make North America the focus of its empire-building efforts

Answers are on pages 140-145

Full-Length Practice Test

Performance Analysis Chart

Directions: Circle the number of each item that you got correct on the Full-length Practice Test. Count how many items you got correct in each row; count how many items you got correct in each column. Write the amount correct per row and column as the numerator in the fraction in the appropriate "Total Correct" box. (The denominators represent the total number of items in the row or column.) Write the grand total correct over the denominator, **64,** at the lower right corner of the chart. (For example, if you got 55 items correct, write *55* so that the fraction reads *55*/**64.**)

Item Type	History (Chapter 2)	Political Science (Chapter 3)	Economics (Chapter 4)	Geography (Chapter 5)	Behavioral Science (Chapter 6)	TOTAL CORRECT
Comprehension	31, 39, 50, 64	34, 36, 60	10, 27, 55	8	13, 61	**/13**
Application	22, 32, 46	15, 16, 17, 18, 54	29, 58, 47	40, 41, 42, 43, 44	6, 25, 48	**/19**
Analysis	19, 20, 30	37, 38, 45, 51	12, 23, 24, 26, 56, 57	9, 28	5, 14, 52, 53	**/19**
Evaluation	1, 2, 11, 21, 33, 49	35	3	7, 63	4, 59, 62	**/13**
TOTAL CORRECT	**/16**	**/13**	**/13**	**/10**	**/12**	**/64**

The chapters named in parentheses indicate where in the *New Revised Cambridge GED Program: Social Studies* you can find specific instruction about each area of Social Studies. You can also find instruction in Unit III Chapter 1 of the *New Revised Cambridge GED Program: Comprehensive Book.*

Simulated Test

Directions: Choose the one best answer for each question.

Time: 85 minutes

Items 1 and 2 are based on the following information.

U.S. government officials have been expressing concern about the federal budget deficit. They are worried because over the years, the government has spent more money than it has taken in. Officials are debating several options to reduce and eventually eliminate the budget deficit.

1. Which of the following is best supported by the information?

(1) Government officials have decided that the budget deficit is here to stay.
(2) Government officials want to eliminate the deficit by pumping more money into the economy.
(3) Government officials do not want the government's expenditures to exceed its revenues.
(4) Borrowing money is a permanent solution to the budget deficit.
(5) The budget deficit problem has been resolved.

2. Which of the following would not be among the options for reducing the budget deficit debated by government officials?

(1) increasing personal and/or corporate income tax rates
(2) charging higher fees for the use of campgrounds in national parks
(3) increasing the defense budget
(4) cutting domestic spending
(5) selling off some government assets

Items 3 and 4 refer to the following cartoon.

©1986, Mike Luckovich, New Orleans Times Picayune. By permission of Mike Luckovick and the Creators Syndicate.

3. According to the 1986 cartoon, the celebration of the Statue of Liberty's centennial was

(1) a period of open immigration
(2) a display of how well the free enterprise system works
(3) viewed as an occasion for profit-making rather than a historical event
(4) a good time to buy souvenirs to remember this event by
(5) undermined by low-cost, imported souvenirs

4. The cartoon could best be used to support the need for more

(1) souvenir stands
(2) job programs for youth
(3) open immigration
(4) understanding of our historical heritage
(5) voter registration drives

Items 5 and 6 refer to the following map.

ROADS AND WATERWAYS BUILT IN THE EARLY 1800s

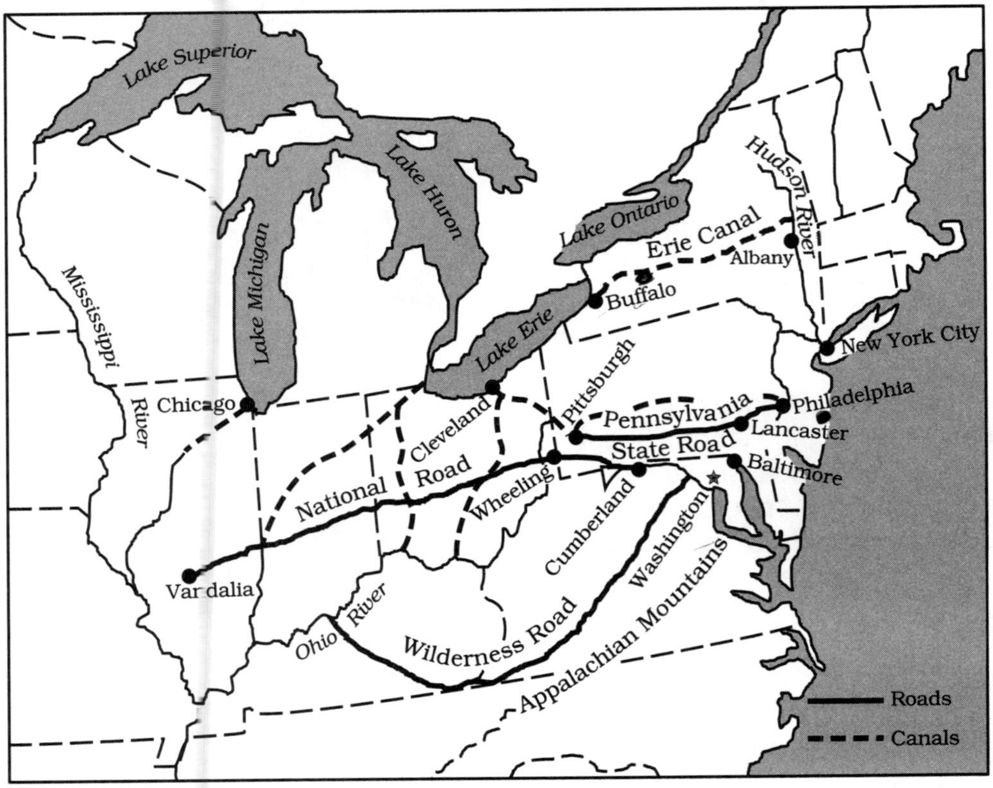

5. The early nineteenth century roads and canals benefited different areas to different extents: New York City probably benefited most directly from the construction of the

(1) canals linking Lake Superior and Lake Michigan
(2) Erie Canal, between Lake Erie and the Hudson River
(3) Pennsylvania State Road
(4) National Road
(5) Wilderness Road

6. Which of the following was least likely to be an effect of the construction of the roads and canals shown in the map?

(1) Produce and other goods became cheaper to transport.
(2) The Ohio River and the Great Lakes became more useful for transportation of goods.
(3) Trade between the North and the South increased.
(4) The area between the Appalachian Mountains and the Mississippi River became more populated.
(5) The American frontier moved westward.

Items 7 to 10 are based on the following information.

Both people and computers use heuristics in searching for solutions to problems. A heuristic is any strategy that can help us solve a problem and thereby reach our goal. Below are five types of heuristics and brief descriptions of what each involves.

(1) means-end—we figure out how distant we are from our goal and then look for ways to reduce this distance
(2) working backward—when we have gotten a result we don't like, we start from this result and go back, step by step, over the process that brought us there, so we can figure out where we went wrong and can avoid the mistake next time
(3) trial and error—we try many different ways to reach the goal, and from each attempt that fails we learn something that may help us with the next attempt
(4) analogous plans—when we know a solution has worked for problems that were similar to our problem, we see if it will work for our problem, too
(5) simplification—we break a complex problem into simple parts, to make it easier to see the solution

Each of the following situations exemplifies the use of a heuristic described above. Choose the one strategy that the example best fits. Each strategy may be used more than once.

7. A scientist is working on a difficult problem. She breaks the problem up into several smaller problems and will begin by solving these. The heuristic used is

(1) means-end
(2) working backward
(3) trial and error
(4) analogous plans
(5) simplification

8. A company's advertising campaign was a complete failure. The company will have to redo it. But, first, the advertising staff thinks through from the way the campaign was conducted, to the analysis that led to the decision to conduct the campaign this way, to the research on which this analysis was based. The head of advertising is determined to find out what went wrong; he doesn't want it to happen again. The heuristic used is

(1) means-end
(2) working backward
(3) trial and error
(4) analogous plans
(5) simplification

9. A food company wants to increase its supermarket sales. It launches a coupons campaign. Then it tries lowering the price of its products. Sales still don't increase. This makes the company think the problem is not a matter of price. Maybe the problem is lack of visibility. The company decides to set up special display cases in supermarkets. If this doesn't work, it has several other ideas to try out. The heuristic used is

(1) means-end
(2) working backward
(3) trial and error
(4) analogous plans
(5) simplification

10. A fast-food chain wants to attract more customers. Several years ago, one of its competitors dramatically upped its sales by introducing a special meal for children. The chain decides that it will advertise a new "Food and Games Box—Just for Kids!" The heuristic used is

(1) means-end
(2) working backward
(3) trial and error
(4) analogous plans
(5) simplification

Item 11 is based on the following graph.

JOBS BY SECTOR (in thousands)

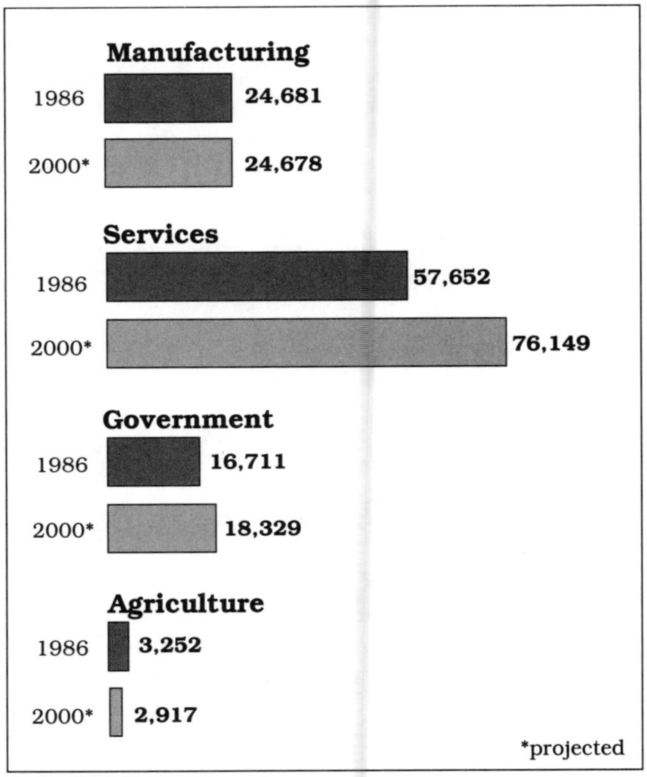

Source: Bureau of Labor Statistics

11. The graph indicates that during the 1990s

(1) many workers will be replaced by machines

(2) all sectors except the service sector will lose jobs

(3) loss of jobs will be greatest in the manufacturing sector

(4) there will be an overall increase in the number of jobs for at least two sectors

(5) the number of jobs will increase more rapidly than the number of workers

---

12. Today the average new home sells for over $100,000. If a family can make a 20 percent down payment on a $100,000 home, they will have to get a mortgage for the remaining $80,000. But banks have income requirements for mortgages: Typically, to get an $80,000 mortgage it's necessary to earn at least $32,000 a year. Many families don't earn nearly this much.

Which of the following conclusions is best supported by the information?

(1) Families who earn less than $32,000 a year cannot buy a home.

(2) Until recently all families were able to afford homes.

(3) Today there are more homeowners than renters.

(4) People will never be able to afford to buy a home.

(5) Some families will have to put off home ownership until their incomes increase.

Item 13 is based on the following cartoon.

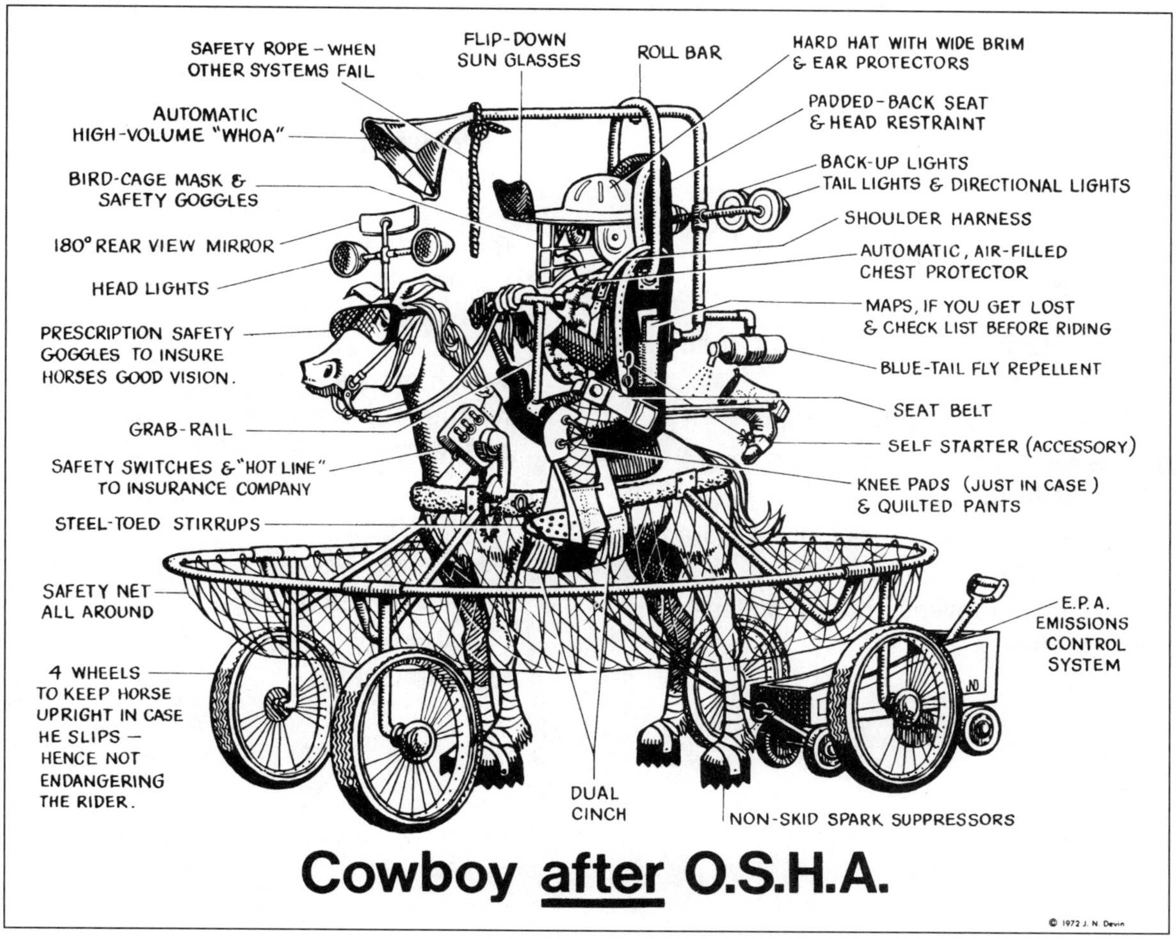

13. The Occupational Safety and Health Administration (OSHA) is a regulatory agency that's part of the Department of Labor. OSHA's main function is to enforce safety codes that protect factory and office workers. The cartoon expresses the opinion that

(1) OSHA regulations should be extended to cowboys and farm workers
(2) it's too soon to judge whether OSHA is doing a good job
(3) OSHA regulations should focus less on office workers and more on factory workers
(4) OSHA regulations are too numerous and complex, and are often unnecessary
(5) OSHA is doing a good job

---

14. Before the 1986 tax reform law there were fifteen tax brackets, with tax rates ranging from 11 to 50 percent. The 1986 law established just two brackets, with a narrower range and overall lower rates. In addition, the law excuses millions of the "working poor" from paying any income taxes.

Based on the information, which of the following is an effect of the 1986 tax reform law?

(1) More people are required to pay taxes.
(2) The government has greatly increased its tax revenues.
(3) The tax structure has become more complex.
(4) The tax burden falls more heavily on the very poor.
(5) Many people are paying lower taxes.

15. The Consumer Price Index measures changes in the cost of goods and services regularly purchased by American families. Upward movement of the index signals an increase in prices; downward movement signals a decrease.

If the Consumer Price Index is up, this means that

(1) American families are making many more purchases
(2) the economy is growing rapidly
(3) the nation is having to import more goods from abroad
(4) American families are getting more for their money
(5) American families are getting less for their money

16. In the northwest of India is the Thar Desert. In the northeast are the Himalayas, some of which are the highest mountains in the world. Down from the Himalayas flows the Ganges River. Thanks to the river, the Ganges Plain is very fertile and supports many people. The Ganges finally empties into the Bay of Bengal. In the South are the Ghats, mountain ranges far lower than the Himalayas.

Which of these geographic features is likely the most directly important to India's economy?

(1) the Thar Desert
(2) the Himalayas
(3) the Ganges River
(4) the Bay of Bengal
(5) the Ghats

17. During the 1880s, state legislatures passed laws regulating the rates charged by cross-country and other railroads. However, in 1886, the Supreme Court declared state regulation of railroad rates unconstitutional.

Which of the following factual statements could have been the grounds for the Supreme Court's decision?

(1) States are required by the Constitution to grant each other's citizens "equal privileges and immunities."
(2) The Eighth Amendment to the Constitution prohibits excessive fines and bail.
(3) The Constitution specifically grants to Congress, rather than the states, the power to regulate all commerce that crosses state boundaries.
(4) All powers not specifically granted to the federal government or prohibited by the Constitution are reserved to the states and the people.
(5) According to the Constitution, states must grant "full faith and credit" to each other's official acts.

18. In his second Inaugural Address, Lincoln said: " With malice toward none, with charity for all..., let us strive on to finish the work we are in; to bind up the nation's wounds."

Lincoln was primarily expressing a desire that

(1) the armies of the North develop more effective fighting tactics
(2) the South be punished for seceding from the Union
(3) blacks be granted full civil rights
(4) the South be reincorporated into the Union, so the nation would again be united
(5) the nation move forward with industrialization, to make up for time lost during the war

Items 19 to 20 are based on the following map.

POPULATION CHANGE IN U.S. METROPOLITAN AREA, 1970-1980
(Changes greater than plus or minus 100,000 people)

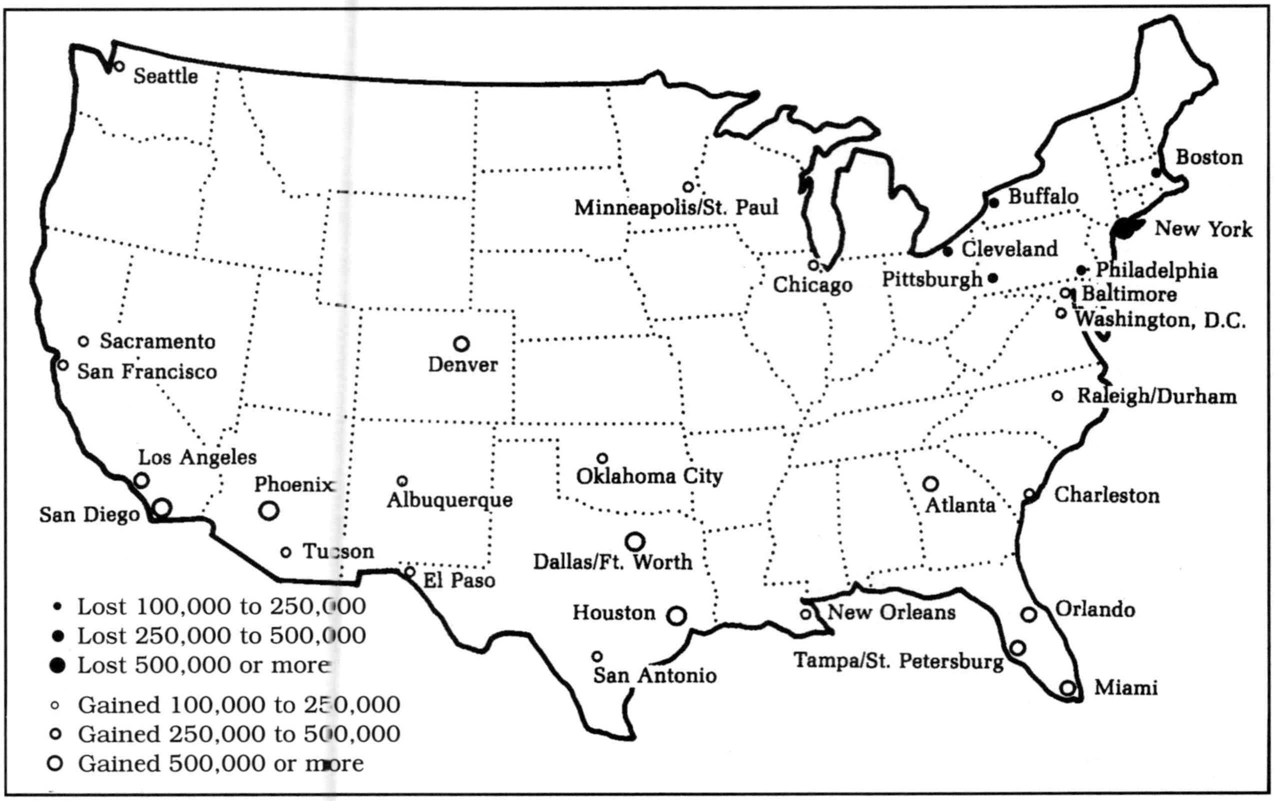

Source: U.S. Census Bureau

19. Of the following cities, which had a moderate gain in population between 1970 and 1980?

(1) New York
(2) Phoenix
(3) San Francisco
(4) Philadelphia
(5) Dallas-Ft. Worth

20. Which of the following statements is supported by information in the map?

(1) Metropolitan areas are spread more or less evenly throughout the United States.
(2) Metropolitan areas that lost population were located mainly in the Northeast.
(3) Metropolitan areas that gained population were located mainly in the Southeast.
(4) Metropolitan areas that gained population did so mainly because of immigration from abroad.
(5) More metropolitan areas lost population than gained population.

Item 21 is based on the following table.

Poverty Rate, by Group
(in percentages)

	Total	White	Black	Hispanic
1959	22.4	18.1	55.1	NA*
1969	12.1	9.5	32.2	NA*
1979	11.6	9.0	31.0	21.8
1985	14.0	11.4	31.3	29.0

*NA = not available

21. For the period shown, which of the following statements is not true?

(1) The greatest gains in fighting poverty came during the 1960s.
(2) The poverty rate for whites was consistently below the national figure.
(3) The poverty rate increased after 1979.
(4) The poverty rate for blacks has not been reduced since 1959.
(5) More than one in 10 people live in poverty.

22. The census, or government count of the population, has a long history. Censuses were conducted in Babylon and China as long ago as 3000 B.C. But censuses were frequently unpopular with ordinary people—and for good reason. Often they revealed which households had property to be taxed or young men who could serve in the army.

Which of the following statements is implied by the passage?

(1) The most thorough censuses were taken in ancient Babylon and China.
(2) Governments have often made use of census information for their own purposes.
(3) Censuses are conducted only by dictatorial governments.
(4) Many countries in the modern world no longer take censuses.
(5) Censuses are necessary only in countries where households tend to be large.

23. The burning of oil, coal, or gas releases carbon dioxide (CO_2) into the atmosphere. CO_2 acts like glass in a greenhouse, so that the earth's atmosphere retains heat that would otherwise be released back into space.

This so-called greenhouse effect has led to a concern that

(1) humans might be using up available supplies of coal, oil, and gas
(2) pollution from the burning of fuels might cause a significant warming of the earth's climate
(3) agricultural products are being contaminated by CO_2
(4) agricultural production in some parts of the world might decrease
(5) space exploration might become impossible

Items 24 to 26 are based on the following information.

Political scientists Angus Campbell, Philip Converse, Warren Miller, and Donald Stokes have said that there are three types of presidential elections.

In maintaining elections the party in power wins because voting patterns have not changed. People vote for the party because they strongly support it and its stands on issues. They will probably continue to vote for the party, and it may stay in power for a decade or more.

In deviating elections the party that has been out of power wins, but voting patterns haven't really changed. Some special factor has caused people to vote for the party out of power in this election. For example, this party might have an especially popular candidate. The party that wins this election probably won't win the next one.

Realigning elections are the third type of elections. In realigning elections the party that has been out of power wins because patterns of voter support have changed. Voters' stands on issues may have shifted in some important way. Sizable groups of people may have joined together behind this party. The party that has just won power can expect to win again.

24. Which of the following election results is the best example of a deviating election?

(1) In 1788 George Washington won the nation's first election.
(2) In 1920 Republican Warren Harding won; his victory began an era of Republican control.
(3) In 1928 Republican Calvin Coolidge won; his victory kept the Republican party in power.
(4) In 1944 Democrat Franklin Roosevelt won his fourth victory in a row.
(5) In 1976 Democrat Jimmy Carter won; however, Republicans won in 1972 and 1980.

25. Which of the following conclusions about election results is supported by the passage?

(1) Election results depend on both long-term voting patterns and immediate issues.
(2) Election results depend mainly on the state of the economy.
(3) Election results depend mainly on how many people vote.
(4) Once out of power, a party has little chance of regaining power.
(5) Third parties are the main factor determining election results.

26. A series of maintaining elections is most likely a sign that

(1) voters are happy with the way things are and with the direction in which the country is moving
(2) the country is going through a period of great change and conflict
(3) the economy is collapsing
(4) there are major disagreements between the president and the Senate
(5) high immigration rates are causing voting patterns to change

Items 27 to 28 are based on the following graph.

WORKERS' AVERAGE WEEKLY EARNINGS

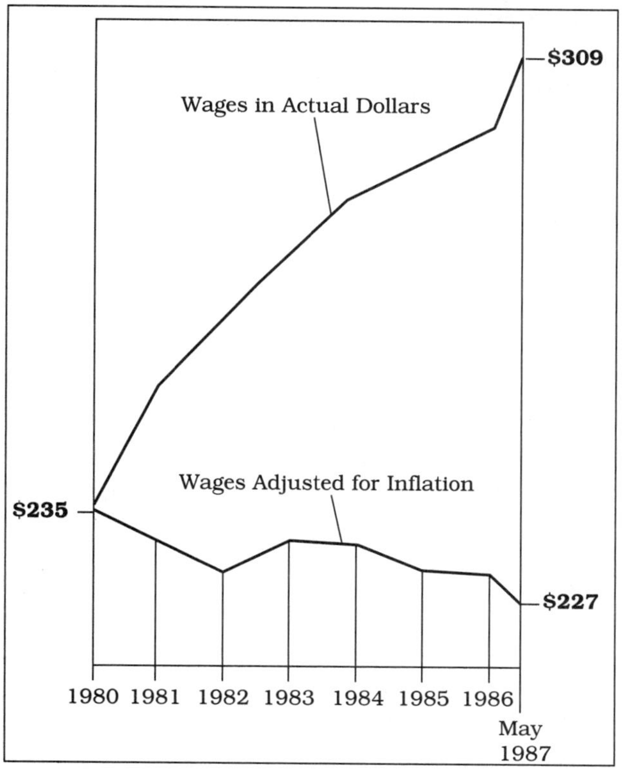

27. Of the following years, in which was workers' buying power weakest because of inflation?

(1) 1980
(2) 1981
(3) 1982
(4) 1983
(5) 1984

28. Which of the following best explains the general decrease over time in workers' adjusted wages?

(1) Wages were taxed more heavily each year.
(2) Annual raises were higher than average to keep up with inflation.
(3) Wages stayed the same, but prices went up.
(4) Wages did not go up as much as prices did.
(5) Wages fell, but prices went up.

---

29. Migration within a country, especially in developing countries, is often hierarchical. This means that people tend to move from smaller places to larger places.

Which of the following would best explain why migration is often hierarchical?

(1) Developed countries tend to have more job opportunities than underdeveloped countries.
(2) Cities tend to have more job opportunities than rural areas.
(3) Cities have many problems that small towns lack.
(4) Modern transportation systems have made migration easier.
(5) Immigration laws differ from country to country.

Items 30 to 33 are based on the following information.

Social scientists have classified the powers described in the U.S. Constitution into five categories. Listed below are the types of constitutional powers and a brief description of each.

(1) delegated powers—powers that are specifically listed in the Constitution and granted to the federal government

(2) implied powers—powers that are exercised by the federal government—even though not specifically listed in the Constitution—because they're needed to carry out powers and duties that are specifically listed

(3) denied powers—powers that the Constitution prohibits government at any levels (state, local, and federal) from exercising

(4) reserved powers—powers that are neither specifically listed nor denied and are therefore considered to belong to the states or the people, and not to the federal government

(5) concurrent powers—powers that are exercised by both the federal government and state governments

Each of the following is an example of one of the powers listed above. Choose the power that best fits the example. The categories may be used more than once in the set of items.

30. Congress establishes a national bank even though the Constitution does not give it the power to do so. However, the Constitution does give Congress the power to collect taxes, coin money, and borrow money. Congress considers a national bank necessary to carrying out these powers. The power described is a(n)

(1) delegated power
(2) implied power
(3) denied power
(4) reserved power
(5) concurrent power

31. The Constitution gives Congress the right to tax citizens. State legislatures are also permitted to levy taxes on their citizens. The power described is a(n)

(1) delegated power
(2) implied power
(3) denied power
(4) reserved power
(5) concurrent power

32. The Bill of Rights forbids the federal government and the states from passing laws that grant people titles of nobility. The power described is a(n)

(1) delegated power
(2) implied power
(3) denied power
(4) reserved power
(5) concurrent power

33. Among other powers, the Constitution authorizes Congress to regulate interstate and foreign commerce, to establish rules for bankruptcy, and to establish post offices. The powers described are

(1) delegated powers
(2) implied powers
(3) denied powers
(4) reserved powers
(5) concurrent powers

34. Several factors influence producers' decisions and options. Generally speaking, the greater the demand for a good or service, the more producers are able to charge. And the lower the price of a good or service, the less of it they're willing to produce.
If wheat commands a higher price than corn, farmers will likely

(1) produce less wheat and more corn
(2) produce more wheat and less corn
(3) charge more for corn
(4) charge less for wheat
(5) try to decrease the demand for corn

<u>Item 35</u> is based on the following cartoon.

© Osrin, *The Cleveland-Plain Dealer,* with permission of the cartoonist.

35. Which of the following statements is best supported by the cartoon?

(1) Big business enjoys an unfair advantage over the average citizen.
(2) The average American is too interested in keeping up with the neighbors.
(3) Most people cannot earn enough money to meet their basic needs.
(4) Increases in wages are barely enough to keep up with increases in prices.
(5) Income is falling behind the rise in the cost of living.

---

36. The "aha" experience—sudden insight into the solution of a problem—often occurs when we are not thinking about the problem at all. Psychologists today understand little more about insight than Louis Pasteur did 100 years ago. Pasteur noted that "chance favors the prepared mind."

By this Pasteur meant that sudden insights into a problem are more likely to occur if an individual

(1) has never before thought about the problem
(2) tends to be lucky in life
(3) has at some earlier point thought a lot about the problem
(4) has studied a great deal of psychology
(5) is too tense to be able to concentrate on the problem

37. In 1939 Congress passed the Hatch Act. This act says that there are certain political activities U.S. government workers cannot engage in. Government workers may vote, but they may not run political campaigns or engage actively in politics.

The Hatch Act was most likely passed in order to

(1) prevent government insiders from having too much influence on elections
(2) extend the political rights of government workers
(3) provide more government jobs
(4) cut back on government bureaucracy and red tape
(5) give government workers a chance to apply their knowledge and experience to politics

<u>Items 38 to 41</u> refer to the following information.

When President Eisenhower left office in 1961, he warned the American people about what he called the military-industrial complex. By that he meant the very close relationship between the companies that produce military weapons and the U.S. Department of Defense.

Until World War II, whenever a war ended, most companies that produced military weapons during the war went back to producing civilian goods. Military weapons were no longer needed. But the end of World War II was different. Cold war tensions arose between the United States and the Soviet Union. Companies therefore kept producing military weapons, and the U.S. government—specifically the Department of Defense—was their main client. This situation was necessary, President Eisenhower explained.

But the military-industrial complex could have dangerous consequences, Eisenhower went on to say. The U.S. government's need for weapons gave companies in the military industry lots of power. And their power was increased by their close relationship to the Department of Defense. The military-industrial complex was powerful enough to have a great deal of influence, Eisenhower concluded. Since the companies would naturally want to sell lots of weapons, for example, defense budgets could wind up being too large. The nation might spend large amounts of money on military projects that were unnecessary and wasteful.

38. Which of the following phrases best summarizes Eisenhower's concern?

(1) Companies producing weapons might have too much weight in government decision-making.
(2) The Soviet Union seemed to be militarily stronger than the United States.
(3) Communists were trying to destroy American institutions.
(4) Congress might not be willing to spend enough money on defense.
(5) There weren't enough companies producing consumer goods.

39. Based on the passage, which of the following best explains the origin of the military-industrial complex?

(1) Congress's unwillingness to spend money on defense
(2) pressure by the United Nations following World War II
(3) the advice of President Eisenhower
(4) hostility between the United States and the Soviet Union
(5) the need to find suitable factory jobs for veterans following World War II

40. Based on the passage, Eisenhower probably held the belief that the military-industrial complex was

(1) an insignificant factor
(2) an out-and-out menace
(3) a Communist plot
(4) a necessary evil
(5) a great blessing

41. Based on the passage, Eisenhower would most likely have approved that

(1) all companies producing weapons switch to producing consumer goods
(2) most military personnel be dismissed to save money
(3) Congress closely examine proposed military budgets to avoid unnecessary spending
(4) the military-industrial complex be given more of a say over foreign policy
(5) the president of a company that makes weapons be chosen as the country's new Secretary of Defense

Item 42 is based on the following time line.

PASSAGE OF CONSTITUTIONAL AMENDMENTS

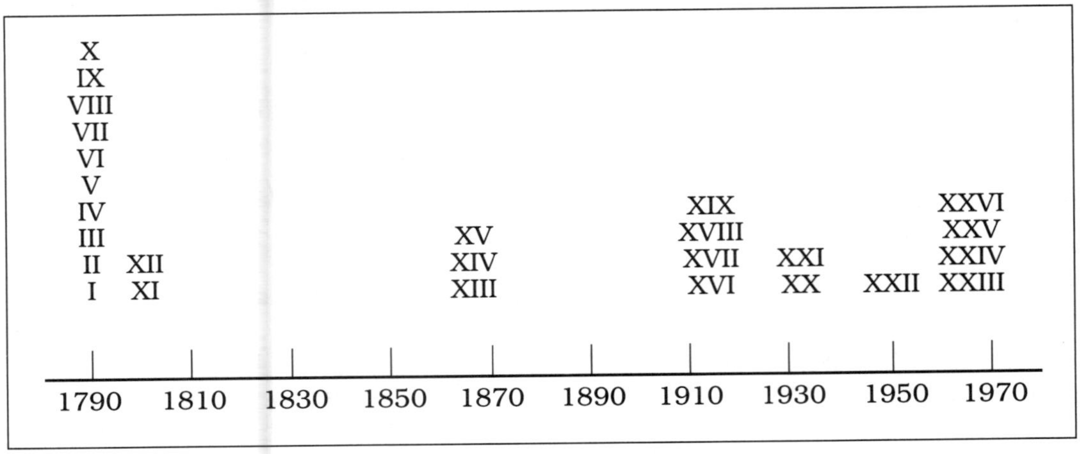

Time Line

42. The time line shows the addition of amendments to the U.S. Constitution. The ten amendments passed in 1790 are the Bill of Rights, which the writers of the Constitution had pledged to add. Which of the following statements is best supported by the figure?

(1) The Constitution has been steadily amended throughout the course of U.S. history.

(2) Amendments have radically changed the Constitution.

(3) Amending the Constitution is an easy process.

(4) Most amendments since the Bill of Rights have been added in the twentieth century.

(5) Most amendments since the Bill of Rights have dealt with extending the vote.

---

43. Medical research sometimes supports the view that mental states have effects on physical ones. Recently, researchers at Ohio State University found that people who feel lonely have significantly lower levels of cells that monitor and destroy cells infected by viruses.

Which of the following best states the main hypothesis that the researchers were testing?

(1) Illness can produce mental states such as loneliness.

(2) Loneliness is the mental state that has the greatest effect on our bodies.

(3) The human body is able to combat viral infections.

(4) The feeling of loneliness lowers the body's resistance to some diseases.

(5) Happy, well-adjusted people are less likely to get sick than others.

Items 44 to 45 are based on the following diagram.

THE MAKING OF U.S. FOREIGN POLICY

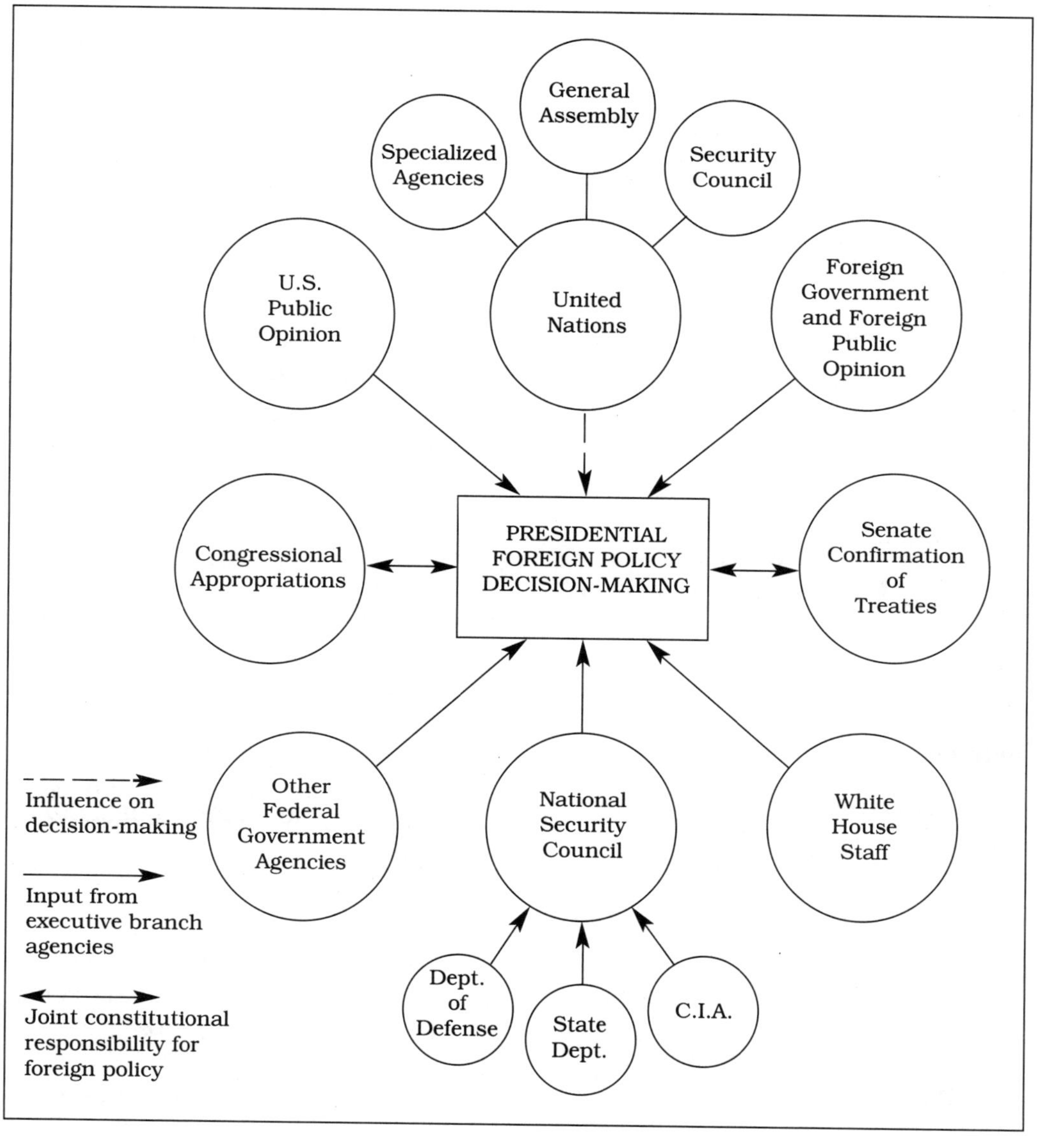

44. Which of the following statements is supported by the chart?

(1) Public opinion can help influence foreign policy decision making.

(2) Foreign policy decisions are usually made by the White House staff.

(3) U.S. foreign policy in recent years has included détente with the Soviet Union.

(4) Appropriations related to foreign policy represent a major part of the U.S. budget.

(5) The Department of Defense has more influence on foreign policy decisions than any other executive branch agency.

45. According to the U.S. Constitutional principle of checks and balances, each of the three branches of government—executive, legislative, and judicial—has powers that limit the powers of the other branches. Which of the following is a way in which foreign policy making reflects the principle of checks and balances?

(1) The president has primary responsibility for foreign policy.
(2) The president consults with leaders of foreign countries.
(3) The United Nations, as the major international organization, has some influence on foreign policy decision making.
(4) Treaties the President makes must be confirmed by the Senate.
(5) Various agencies from the executive branch contribute to foreign policy making.

Item 46 is based on the following graph.

**THE UNITED STATES
JUST BEFORE THE CIVIL WAR**

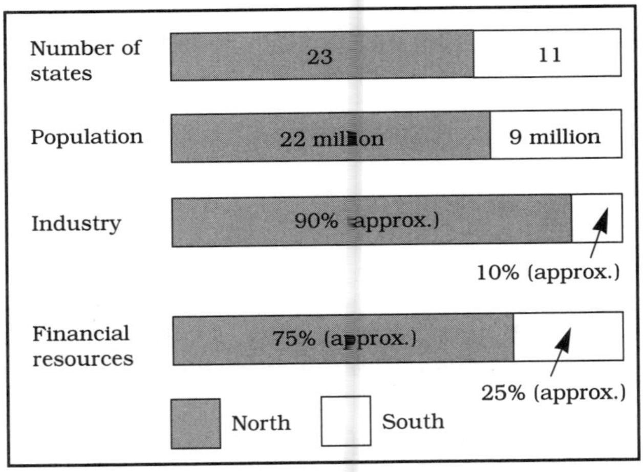

46. Which of the following can be inferred from the graph?

(1) The North and the South were so evenly balanced that a long, drawn-out struggle was inevitable.
(2) The South was in a better position than the North as long as the struggle could be quickly resolved.
(3) The North had significant advantages over the South, especially the resources for a prolonged struggle.
(4) The South had the significant advantage of being more familiar with the terrain where the war was fought.
(5) The South was so lacking in resources that Southern victory was impossible.

---

47. To become law a bill must be signed by the President. The President does not, however, have the power to edit bills. He must accept the entire bill or veto it. When Congress sends the President a bill that is of real importance to him/her, it will often attach "riders." Riders are measures Congress favors that are unrelated to the main bill.

Based on the information, which of the following statements best explains why Congress uses riders?

(1) Congress doesn't always have time to write separate bills.
(2) Congress wants the president to edit bills.
(3) Congress wants the riders to be vetoed.
(4) Congress can get the President to approve of measures he/she might otherwise reject.
(5) Congress wants to show its support for the president.

Items 48 to 51 are based on the following information.

Metallic and nonmetallic minerals—copper, lead, sulfur, etc.—are a very important kind of natural resource. Such minerals cannot be considered plentiful: They make up less than 1 percent of the earth's crust. And, because they were formed by geologic processes, they are by no means evenly distributed among nations. A country like the United States that covers a wide area is most likely to have ample and varied mineral resources.

In fact, the United States is among the leading producers of minerals. A few decades ago the United States was self-sufficient in minerals. Today, however, it must depend heavily on a number of other countries.

The United States is not just a leading producer of minerals; it is also a leading consumer. When industrial and other uses are taken into account, the average American "consumes" about 40,000 pounds of minerals a year.

Because of consumption in the United States and around the world, the earth's mineral supply is being depleted. Some minerals can no longer be found in "high grade" deposits, or deposits that are easy to reach and mine. These deposits have been used up. Remaining deposits of such minerals can be mined only with new technologies and at great cost.

48. The mineral shortage that the United States is now experiencing is mostly due to

(1) the fact that the nation never had rich supplies of mineral resources
(2) international political conflicts that have blocked supplies
(3) Americans' heavy consumption of mineral resources in the past
(4) a lack of scientific research into substitutes for minerals
(5) the fact that minerals are not distributed evenly throughout the country

49. Which of the following could have the greatest negative effect on efforts to conserve mineral resources?

(1) recycling of mineral resources
(2) industrial use of mineral substitutes
(3) rapid population increases
(4) discovery of new mineral deposits
(5) development of new mineral substitutes

50. According to the information, the countries most likely to have a wide range of mineral resources are those that

(1) are located in the Northern Hemisphere
(2) are the largest consumers of mineral resources
(3) are large in size
(4) have the most varied landforms
(5) have similar terrain throughout

51. The information implies that in our time the earth's mineral resources

(1) have been used up
(2) have increased because of technology
(3) have become relatively expensive to obtain
(4) have become cheaper to obtain
(5) are still plentiful

<u>Items 52 to 55</u> are based on the following graph.

AGE DISTRIBUTION IN THE UNITED STATES

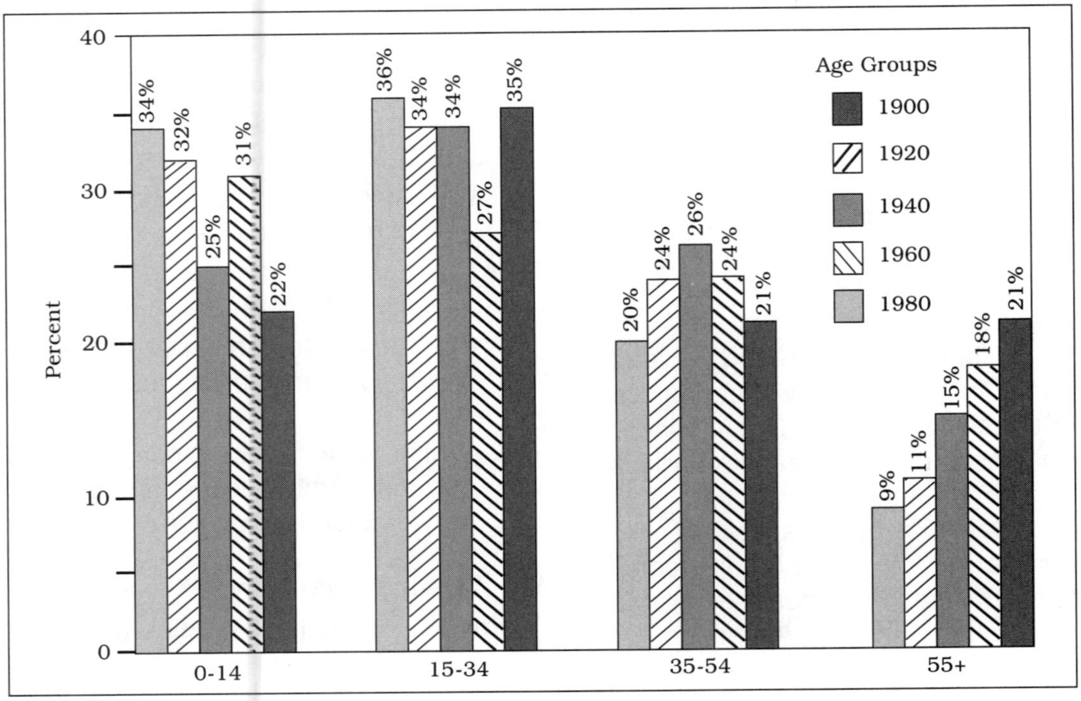

52. Of the years shown, the year in which the 0–14 age group contained the smallest percentage of the population was

(1) 1900
(2) 1920
(3) 1940
(4) 1960
(5) 1980

53. Based on the graph, which of the following statements is true?

(1) In 1920, the 55+ age group was the largest of the four age groups.
(2) In 1960, the 0–14 age group was the smallest of the four age groups.
(3) Throughout the period shown, the 15–34 age group has tended to be small compared to the other groups.
(4) The 0–14 age group contained exactly the same percentage of the population in 1980 as it did in 1900.
(5) The 35–54 age group contained a greater percentage of the population in 1940 than it did in the other years shown.

54. Compared to 1900, excluding the 15–34 age group, the U.S. population in 1980 was

(1) wealthier
(2) older
(3) younger
(4) larger
(5) smaller

55. If the trend shown in the graph continues, the United States will probably have to

(1) build more health care facilities
(2) create jobs for a rapidly growing workforce
(3) construct new housing to avoid sudden, severe shortages
(4) build new elementary and junior high schools
(5) construct more federal prisons

Items 56 to 59 are based on the following information.

There are many different approaches the government can take when making decisions about the economy. Listed below are five types of approaches with a brief description of each.

(1) Laissez-faire—the economy can and should regulate itself; government action, generally speaking, will have only undesirable results.

(2) Monetarism—the amount of money in circulation is the main factor determining the performance of the economy; government action should be focused on, and limited to, regulating the growth of the money supply.

(3) Supply-side—the performance of the economy depends on companies having the incentive to produce and the income to invest; government action should focus on insuring that these conditions are met.

(4) Keynesian—the economy cannot simply regulate itself, in periods of economic difficulty, government might need to stimulate the economy through borrowing and through spending— for example, on programs that provide employment.

(5) Marxist—both economic performance and social justice depend on the government running the economy and owning and operating most, if not all, businesses.

Each of the following examples is based on one of the types of economic approaches described above. Choose the type of approach that best fits the example. The types may be used more than once in the set of items.

56. An economist criticizes the government for spending too much and for failing to have the central bank follow a policy to make sure that money supply targets were set and met. The type of approach this economist advocates is most likely

(1) laissez-faire
(2) monetarist
(3) supply-side
(4) Keynesian
(5) Marxist

57. In a time of deepening depression and numerous business closings, a presidential administration decides to take a range of actions and to spend money on an extensive program to give work to the unemployed. The type of approach the administration is following is most likely

(1) laissez-faire
(2) monetarist
(3) supply-side
(4) Keynesian
(5) Marxist

58. Congress passes a law cutting tax rates. Reductions for businesses are especially large. The hope is that if companies can hold onto more of their profits, they will be motivated to produce more and to reinvest the profits they've held onto. The type of approach that this legislation is based on is most likely

(1) laissez-faire
(2) monetarist
(3) supply-side
(4) Keynesian
(5) Marxist

59. Despite strong calls for restricting imports to protect American jobs, the president decides it's better not to take any action. Although inefficient firms will go under, efficient competitors and consumers will benefit, he argues. The type of approach the president advocates is most likely

(1) laissez-faire
(2) monetarist
(3) supply-side
(4) Keynesian
(5) Marxist

Items 60 to 61 are based on the following information.

In February 1967, Martin Luther King, Jr., declared, "The promises of the Great Society have been shot down on the battlefield of Vietnam."

Like many other clergy and citizens, King also saw the conduct of the war as a moral issue. American air attacks devastated the Vietnamese countryside. More explosives fell on Vietnam than were used on all of Europe and Asia in World War II. Planes sprayed chemicals on the forests and farmland of South Vietnam to destroy the enemy's hiding places and food supplies. Many critics also had moral objections to the government of Nguyen Van Thieu, who was elected president of South Vietnam in 1967. To them, Thieu seemed as much a brutal dictator as were the communists.

(Am. Journey, PH. p. 589)

60. King's opposition to the Vietnam War was based on his belief that

(1) unpopular governments must sometimes be removed through war
(2) war is an unavoidable evil
(3) nothing justifies the destruction of people's lives, their property, and the natural resources they depend on to survive
(4) freedom must be defended at whatever cost or destruction of life, property, or natural resources
(5) war is against the will of God and humanity

61. Because Dr. King strongly valued freedom, which of the following would you expect him to support?

(1) the Chinese government's killing of students during their protest for democratic reforms in Tiananmen Square in 1989
(2) the imprisonment of Nelson Mandela for his opposition to the white South African government's policy of Apartheid (separation of the races)
(3) the military overthrow of popularly elected Haitian President Aristide in 1991
(4) the U.S. invasion of the Caribbean island of Granada to combat Cuban influence
(5) the break up of the Soviet Union into separate, autonomous countries forming the Commonwealth of Independent States

Item 62 is based on the following graph.

62. Much of the trash that people litter on the beach ends up in the ocean killing wildlife. Why is the single, largest source of sea and shore trash dangerous to wildlife?

(1) Glass cuts the gills of fish.
(2) Big fish and birds get caught around the necks in car tires.
(3) Fish and birds die after swallowing balloons and plastic bags.
(4) Dolphins and turtles choke on metal beverage cans.
(5) Birds, dolphins, and large fish die from ingesting paper products.

Items 63 to 64 are based on the following information.

No issue has stirred stronger debate than whether women should have the right to end a pregnancy through abortion. In 1973, in the case of Roe v. Wade, the Supreme Court voted 7 to 2 to allow abortion in certain cases. The Constitution, the Court stated, included a right of privacy for all Americans. Under that right, women were free to decide whether to bear an unborn child—at least during the first three months of pregnancy.

A stormy debate has raged ever since. On one side are "pro-life" activists. They have argued that unborn children have the right to live from the moment in which they are conceived.

On the other side are "pro-choice" activists. They argue that an unborn fetus is not a baby, especially in the early stages of its growth.

In 1989, the Supreme Court moved slightly away from Roe v. Wade in Webster v. Reproductive Health Services. That case gave individual states the option of placing stiffer restrictions on abortions.

(Am. Journey, PH, p. 682)

63. Which of the following statements is an opinion?

(1) Abortion is murder of an unborn child.
(2) Webster v. Reproductive Health Services restricts a woman's right to have an abortion.
(3) Roe v. Wade legalized abortions during the first trimester of pregnancy.
(4) Abortion is a controversial issue in the U.S.
(5) Presidents Reagan and Bush publicly voiced their opposition to abortion.

64. Which of the following would not be a result of the Supreme Court's ruling in Webster v. Reproductive Health Services and the abortion debate?

(1) an increase in "pro-choice" lobbying
(2) an increase of "pro-life" demonstrations
(3) some states limiting a woman's right to have a legal abortion
(4) more women having legal abortions nationwide
(5) abortion as a campaign issue in the 1992 Presidential election

Answers are on pages 145–150.

Simulated Practice Test

Performance Analysis Chart

Directions: Circle the number of each item that you got correct on the Simulated Practice Test. Count how many items you got correct in each row; count how many items you got correct in each column. Write the amount correct per row and column as the numerator in the fraction in the appropriate "Total Correct" box. (The denominators represent the total number of items in the row or column.) Write the grand total correct over the denominator, **64,** at the lower right corner of the chart. (For example, if you got 55 items correct, write *55* so that the fraction reads *55***/64.**)

Item Type	History (Chapter 2)	Political Science (Chapter 3)	Economics (Chapter 4)	Geography (Chapter 5)	Behavioral Science (Chapter 6)	TOTAL CORRECT
Comprehension	3, 5, 18, 38	13	11, 27	19, 50	21, 36, 52, 53	**/13**
Application	41, 61	24, 30, 31, 32, 33, 45	2, 34, 56, 57, 58, 59		7, 8, 9, 10, 55	**/19**
Analysis	6, 14, 39, 46, 63, 64	26, 37, 47	15, 28	23, 29, 48, 51, 62	22, 43, 54	**/19**
Evaluation	4, 40, 42, 60	17, 25, 44	1, 12, 35	16, 20, 49		**/13**
TOTAL CORRECT	**/16**	**/13**	**/13**	**/10**	**/12**	**/64**

The chapters named in parentheses indicate where in the *New Revised Cambridge GED Program: Social Studies* you can find specific instruction about each area of Social Studies. You can also find instruction in Unit III Chapter 1 of the *New Revised Cambridge GED Program: Comprehensive Book.*

Answers and Explanations

History Items

1. **(2)** *Comprehension/History.* Both first-wave and second-wave immigrants came to America to escape poverty and/or religious oppression in their homelands. All the other choices are differences between the two groups of immigrants.
2. **(1)** *Application/History.* The Russians were part of the second wave of immigrants. These immigrants came at the end of the nineteenth century, settled in cities, and often worked in low-paying factory jobs. The other immigrants mentioned came at different times and/or mainly worked in other occupations.
3. **(3)** *Analysis/History.* First-wave immigrants contributed to westward expansion, and second-wave immigrants contributed to industrialization. Westward expansion and industrialization were two of the key processes that built America. Therefore, it can be said that by contributing to these processes, immigrants helped build America. Choice (4) is not mentioned in the passage. The other choices, although mentioned or implied, don't explain how immigrants contributed to building America.
4. **(1)** *Comprehension/History.* Territories were not allowed to participate in elections. (Note that the shading of the territories doesn't correspond to any of the candidates in the map legend.) Thus, they couldn't have determined the election outcome. All the other statements are true.
5. **(5)** *Analysis/History.* In the election of 1860, Lincoln took the West and the North while Breckinridge, the Southern Democrat candidate, carried the South. Voting clearly took place along regional lines. Choice (1) is contradicted since more than two parties ran candidates. Choice (2) is not supported, since Lincoln, the winner, had a clear majority of electoral votes. Choice (3) is contradicted, since Lincoln had an electoral majority and a popular majority. Nothing in the map or legend relates to choice (4).
6. **(2)** *Application/History.* Searches and seizures could violate the privacy of one's home. Choice (1) is inappropriate since representation was not the issue of the searches. Choices (3) and (4) are both too general. Choice (5) is unrelated to search and seizure.
7. **(2)** *Evaluation/History.* Voters in the eight royal colonies (more than half of the colonies) could elect only members of the lower house of the legislature. That implies that these legislatures had two houses, upper and lower. Choices (1) and (3) are explicitly contradicted by information given. There is no indication in the passage about when legislatures were formed (5) or whether colonists voted for Members of Parliament (4).
8. **(2)** *Evaluation/History.* Self-governing colonies elected both governors and legislators, proprietary colonies elected all legislators, and royal colonies elected only some legislators. Therefore, the three kinds of colonies differed in the amount of democracy they enjoyed. Choice (1) is wrong, since colonists had experience with voting. Choice (3) is contradicted by the fact that there were legislators as well as governors. Choice (4) is wrong since the passage mentions eligible voters, which implies that there were some colonists who were not eligible voters. Choice (5) is wrong since taxes are not mentioned.
9. **(2)** *Analysis/History.* The map shows that the westernmost part of the border between the United States and Canada was established by treaty in 1846. Choice (2) is therefore correct, and choice (1) must be wrong. Since the treaty line of 1846 is between the United States and Canada, choice (4) is unlikely. Choice (5) is wrong since the map shows that the area known as Oregon Country was divided between the United States and Canada. Choice (3) can be eliminated, since the map shows that in 1846 Mexico still had territory in what is now the United States.
10. **(4)** *Analysis/History.* The Federalists would have objected to measures that shifted power to state and local governments because they wanted the national

government to be much stronger than the state governments. Choices (1) and (5) are in keeping with the Federalist position that democracy should be limited. Choices (2) and (3), which helped manufacturers and bankers, would also have been supported by the Federalists.

11. **(1)** *Evaluation/History.* Since each state made up its own regulations and tariffs, these were very unlikely to be the same from state to state. The statements in the other choices, in contrast, all fit with the situation in which each state did as it pleased and Congress had no power to regulate trade.

12. **(3)** *Comprehension/History.* John Adams states that if a debate on voter qualification were opened, women might demand to be given the vote. Thus, it can be assumed that at the time of the quote women were unable to vote. Choice (2) is explicitly contradicted by the information. None of the other choices is supported.

13. **(4)** *Analysis/History.* John Adams speaks against any moves to allow new groups to vote. He mentions several groups (women, youths, the poor) and implies that it wouldn't make sense for them to participate in government. He mentions distinctions and differing ranks in society and indicates he wants these to remain. All this supports choice (4). Since Adams didn't want changes or greater democracy, choices (2), (3), and (5) are incorrect. The quote says nothing about slavery, as in choice (1).

14. **(5)** *Comprehension/History.* The cartoon indicates that the enactment of civil rights legislation has been a difficult and important step: The civil rights bill is standing on a mountain peak labeled "enactment in law." But now that the bill's been enacted in law, it's got to reach the goal of "fulfillment in spirit." This goal, as the sign and the trail indicate, is still a long way off. Choice (3) cannot be the message of the cartoon, since full civil rights requires fulfillment in spirit. There is nothing in the cartoon related to the more specific statements in choices (1), (2), and (4).

15. **(5)** *Comprehension/History.* The passage is mainly concerned with explaining factors that led white Southerners to uphold the institution of slavery. The topics in choices (1), (2), and (3) are not discussed. Although the topic in choice (4) <u>is</u> discussed, it's simply part of the larger, more general topic.

16. **(2)** *Evaluation/History.* This explanation is sociological and psychological because it has to do with social classes and with people's thoughts and feelings. Slavery, in effect, gave many nonslaveholders someone to look down on and allowed them to identify with the wealthy Southerners. The statement in choice (1) was not a reason at all, but simply an argument used by some Southerners to defend slavery. Choice (3), although discussed in the passage, is an <u>economic</u> explanation. Choice (4) is not discussed. Choice (5) states a fact mentioned in the passage but does not offer an explanation for why slavery continued.

17. **(4)** *Comprehension/History.* The caption "It's going to be just turned around" seems to be the cartoonist's response to objections to the proposed law, in particular to objections that the new law might be discriminatory. Selection always went on, the cartoonist is claiming, but now, with the quota system, the entire process will be much more efficient. Note the contrast between the disorder in the lefthand drawing and the order in the righthand drawing where the funnel has been reversed. Choices (2) and (3) must therefore be wrong, since the cartoonist favors the new law. Choices (1) and (5) don't deal with the real subject matter of the cartoon.

18. **(4)** *Analysis/History.* Since the cotton gin made it much easier and cheaper to process cotton, it allowed the South to produce much more cotton than before. Choices (1), (2), and (5) describe effects opposite to actual events: Large cotton plantations became possible, more land could be cultivated, and some farmers switched <u>to</u> cotton cultivation. Choice (3) is not supported by the passage, which indicates that Southerners became users, not exporters, of a new kind of machinery.

19. **(4)** *Comprehension/History.* The passage shows how population patterns, social class structure, work, homes, and lifestyles changed as more and more Americans lived in cities. The other choices, while all stated or implied by the passage, all concern details. Only choice (4) summarizes the main point.

20. **(2)** *Analysis/History.* Much of the passage is devoted to discussing problems that accompanied urbanization—pollution, poverty, crowding, etc. However, the passage does not imply that urbanization was unnecessary, as in choice (1). Nor does it discuss immediate benefits of

urbanization, as in choice (3). While urbanization may in fact have made the United States prosperous, as in choice (4), such an effect is not discussed in the passage. Contrary to choice (5), the passage says that urbanization has a very significant impact.

21. **(4)** *Analysis/History.* The passage states that in rural areas there were few differences in wealth, but in cities large economic classes developed. Choices (1) and (5) are contradicted. Nothing is said about the middle class, as in choice (2). Choice (3) cannot be correct, since the upper class grew in size.

22. **(2)** *Analysis/History.* The graph shows that the number of farm laborers dropped significantly over the 1950s. Choice (1) is therefore wrong. Choice (3) is also wrong, both because total output went up, so more goods were being produced, and because production per man-hour went up, so the technology was making it easier for farm workers to produce goods. Choices (4) and (5) are not addressed by the graph.

23. **(1)** *Analysis/History.* Choice (1) is supported by the rises in total farm output and production per man-hour. Choices (4) and (5) are contradicted by the rise in total farm output. There is nothing in the graph about quality or exports to support choice (2) or choice (3).

24. **(4)** *Application/History.* The War on Poverty emphasized helping people to help themselves. The programs in choices (1), (2), (3), and (5), in keeping with this emphasis, give people a "hand." Those in choice (4), in contrast, are providing a "hand-out."

25. **(5)** *Application/History.* The statements in choices (1)–(4) all involve expanding democracy: More people are given the vote, they are allowed to vote more often, and they vote for a wider range of officials than before. Choice (5), in contrast, has to do with voting patterns, and not with the expansion of democracy.

26. **(1)** *Evaluation/History.* The passage indicates that these reformers looked at a wide range of problems, and it implies that they were among the early reformers. Therefore, it's likely that the reformers helped to draw attention to social problems. Given the limitations of these reformers, choices (2), (3), and (5) can all be ruled out. Nothing in the information relates to choice (4).

27. **(2)** *Application/History.* Reformers thought problems were caused by the weakness of individuals. They accordingly blamed factory workers' problems on their drinking and attempted to discourage workers from drinking. Since the reformers did <u>not</u> try to change society and its laws, all the other choices can be eliminated.

28. **(4)** *Analysis/History.* The information states that the British felt the colonists had not shared the costs of the French and Indian War. The measures discussed all involved either taxing the colonists or forcing the colonists to meet the needs of British troops. It can therefore be concluded that these measures attempted to get colonists to pay for their defense by British troops. Choices (2), (3), and (5) are each in some way contradicted by the information. Nothing is said to support choice (1).

29. **(3)** *Comprehension/History.* The Sugar, Stamp, and Townshend Acts were all taxes. Both the Sugar Act and the Townshend Acts taxed imports. Only the Stamp Act was a tax on materials that were produced and distributed within the colonies themselves.

30. **(4)** *Analysis/History.* The information indicates that the measures were strongly opposed by the colonists and implies that this opposition helped lead to the American Revolution. Choice (1) cannot be right, since the measures were passed after the French and Indian War. Choice (2) is contradicted since relations worsened. Nothing is said to support choices (3) or (5).

31. **(4)** *Comprehension/History.* Friedan argued that women wanted the opportunity to do a range of different things with their lives, rather than just being confined to the role of homemaker.

32. **(2)** *Comprehension/History.* Friedan and the other founders of the National Organization for Women felt that women were dissatisfied with their lives and that it was necessary to obtain full equality for women. Choice (3) involves a detail from the passage and is not a summary. The other choices are contradicted by or not mentioned in the passage.

33. **(4)** *Analysis/History.* The passage says that truly restrictive laws had already been changed. Therefore, choices (1)–(3) are wrong. At the time the book was written, women already had the right to vote. It also says that women did not have full equality and women's roles in society

were limited, especially in the area of careers. Therefore, choice (5) is also unlikely.

34. **(1)** *Application/History.* Choice (1) involves removing legal barriers to equality, which is one of the aims of the National Organization for Women. Choice (2) is incorrect, since women had the right to vote long before the 1960s. None of the other choices are in keeping with the aims of the organization, as expressed in the passage.

35. **(5)** *Evaluation/History.* The cartoon shows Uncle Sam (the U.S.) trying to help plow the rocky soil of Latin America. Before plowing can be effective, such "stones" as poverty and illiteracy must be removed. Thus the cartoon explains a reason behind the Alliance for Progress Program, in which the United States offered aid to Latin American countries that undertook social and economic reforms.

Geography Items

1. **(3)** *Application/Geography.* Since oil, like coal, is a substance from nature, burning oil instead of coal would not be an example of conservation. All the other choices in some way conserve natural resources.

2. **(3)** *Application/Geography.* Since a toxic waste dump is the result of human activity rather than nature, an area with such a dump is not an example of an environment with a natural hazard.

3. **(3)** *Comprehension/Geography.* People tend to use their experience to convince themselves that the odds of anything happening to them are very low. None of the other choices are offered as explanations.

4. **(5)** *Comprehension/Geography.* The "Air Pollution Sources" figure shows that 63 percent of air pollution comes from either transportation or the burning of fuel in stationary sources, that is, homes and offices. Choice (1) cannot be supported, since the graphs do not report on other forms of pollution. Contrary to choice (2), the graphs don't show where carbon monoxide comes from. Choice (3) is wrong, since hydrocarbons account for only 15 percent of air pollution. Similarly, miscellaneous sources, in choice (4), account for only 10 percent of all sources.

5. **(5)** *Evaluation/Geography.* If each area can support only a certain, limited number of people, then the earth as a whole cannot support an unlimited number of people. The earth can support only as many people as all its regions can support. All the other choices are consistent with the information.

6. **(5)** *Comprehension/Geography.* In Zaire, only 3% of the land is used as farmland. The other countries listed all use a larger percentage of their land as farmland.

7. **(2)** *Evaluation/Geography.* Canada is the second largest country listed under Total Area, yet it is <u>second to the least</u> in terms of farmland with only 7%. The other four countries are large and all have a large amount of farmland.

8. **(1)** *Evaluation/Geography.* Australia has by far the smallest population of the countries in the table, yet in amount of farmland it is second only to the Soviet Union. Thus, Australia is the most likely to be relatively self-sufficient in food and the least likely to need to import large quantities of food.

9. **(2)** *Application/Geography.* The action by the sea is a natural process, and it has the effect over time of reducing the amount of land. None of the other choices fit both parts of the definition of gradational processes.

10. **(5)** *Comprehension/Geography.* The map shows how much of the food moderately active people require is available in each Asian country. The map does not show how many hungry people there are, choice (4), nor does it reveal anything about the topics mentioned in the other choices.

11. **(3)** *Evaluation/Geography.* China and the Commonwealth of Independent States, in choices (2) and (5), do not lack land. Laos and Bangladesh, in choices (1) and 4), lack land, but they also have a limited food supply. Japan is a small country with a high calorie supply per person. It is the only country that could be used to make the argument that a small country doesn't necessarily have a limited food supply.

12. **(2)** *Comprehension/Geography.* Three places listed receive more rainfall than Key West: Hartford, Montgomery, and Mount Waialeale. Of those, only Hartford and Montgomery have humid climates.

13. **(5)** *Analysis/Geography.* According to the classification, the area with the least amount of rainfall, less than 4" annually,

is the desert. Neither hot nor cold climates are necessarily dry which eliminates choices (1) and (3). The desert located in high altitudes may have cool temperatures. Choice (4) is also incorrect: The desert is dryer than an arid area.

14. **(3)** *Evaluation/Geography.* A majority of the places shown fall into the humid climate range of 20–60" of rainfall. Furthermore, these places are located in many different areas of the country (the Northeast, Southeast, Midwest, and Northwest). Therefore it appears that much of the United States has a humid climate, as in choice (3). Choice (1) is not supported since the information says nothing about temperatures. Contrary to choice (5), the Southeast and Southwest are shown to have very different levels of rainfall.
15. **(4)** *Analysis/Geography.* Continentality affects temperature by producing rapid heat loss. Therefore, it is likely that the Commonwealth of Independent States has long, cold winters. Since rapid heat loss is a feature of continentality, the area is not likely to have a hot, desert-like climate, as in choice (1), or year-around mild weather, as in choice (3). Since the effect in terms of precipitation is that the air is dry, the area is not likely to have a humid, tropical climate, as in choice (2), or long periods of heavy rainfall, as in choice (5).
16. **(1)** *Analysis/Geography.* If Britain is about the same distance from the equator but not characterized by continentality, its climate should be warmer than the former Soviet Union's and less dry. Therefore choice (1) is correct and the other choices can be eliminated.
17. **(4)** *Comprehension/Geography.* There is only one difference between the two figures. In the figure showing the inversion, there is a layer of warmer air between the warm surface air and the cool air. As the figures shows, this warmer air causes pollution to be trapped and therefore to become worse.
18. **(3)** *Comprehension/Geography.* The passage focuses on how the earth, which is a sphere, can be represented on a flat map and on the reasons for, and results of, doing so. The ideas in choices (1), (2), and (5) are mentioned only briefly or not at all.
19. **(3)** *Evaluation/Geography.* The passage states that different projections are used because different kinds of distortions are acceptable depending on the purpose of the map. This must mean that different projections result in different distortions. Choice (4) is specifically contradicted in the text. Choice (1) is incorrect, since shape can be accurately represented on maps; but not on a map that accurately represents the other three features. Choice (2) is contradicted in the passage, which states that all maps distort at least one of the four features. Choice (5) is also contradicted, since the passage states that maps are much easier to use and store than globes.
20. **(1)** *Application/Geography.* The Southeast is the only area which shows no banking problems for both 1989 and 1990 and has a hot climate year round. The Caribbean islands are just south of Florida, the southernmost state in the Southeast. The Southwest and the West show banking problems in both years. The Midwest and Mid-Atlantic areas do not have a warm climate all year, nor are they located near the Caribbean.

Economics Items

1. **(1)** *Evaluation/Economics.* Even though they are small, unions are strong because they are concentrated in one part of the economy. But because of that concentration, when that part of the economy suffers, unions suffer much more than they would if they were more evenly spread out.
2. **(2)** *Analysis/Economics.* The information indicates that unions have been hurt because the manufacturing sector has been hurt. The layoff of a significant number of manufacturing workers would be a likely result of problems in the manufacturing sector. Layoffs could lead to a drop in union membership. There is nothing in the information to support any of the other choices.
3. **(4)** *Application/Economics.* Since the advertising slogan in choice (4) refers to a negative (no trimmings) connected with the product itself, rather than with the competitors', it best applies the findings of the study. The slogan in choice (1) reflects the original negative advertising approach that the study rejected. The slogans in the other choices use other approaches.

4. **(2)** *Analysis/Economics.* Since 88 percent of all business earnings go to one type of business, those businesses must be either large or numerous in order to claim so much of the available income. Choice (2), therefore, offers an explanation for the difference in businesses' earning rates. The fact in choice (1) cannot explain why corporations should earn most of the income. Choices (3)–(5) have little, if anything, to do with the earnings of the different kinds of businesses.

5. **(3)** *Application/Economics.* A person who quits a job, as in choice (3), is frictionally unemployed. Choice (1) does not fall into any of the unemployment categories. Choices (2), (4), and (5) are examples of seasonal unemployment, cyclical unemployment and structural unemployment, in that order.

6. **(2)** *Application/Economics.* When an industry experiences technological changes, the loss of jobs affects the entire industry. The structurally unemployed worker likely will not find a similar job elsewhere or in the future. That person should retrain. Except in isolated cases, retraining is appropriate only when a certain type of job ceases to exist. Therefore, none of the other choices are correct.

7. **(4)** *Application/Economics.* Most lifeguards become unemployed at the end of the summer. Their unemployment is seasonal.

8. **(2)** *Application/Economics.* No matter how bad the economy is, surgeons will still be needed. They provide an essential service and are not likely to become cyclically unemployed. In contrast, if the economy is bad and people are spending less, fewer appliances, cars, clothes, and books may be sold. The workers in choices (1), (3), (4), and (5) are more likely to be affected by cyclical unemployment.

9. **(5)** *Comprehension/Economics.* The table compares three groups of working mothers to all mothers in the same groups. The percentages show that in each year reported, a larger proportion of all mothers in each group works. The table has no information about any of the other choices.

10. **(1)** *Analysis/Economics.* As more mothers of young children enter the labor force, more children will likely spend time in child care. Choices (2), (3), and (4) are not related to the information in the table. Although choice (5) may be represented in the table, there is no way to know from the information in the table whether the group is increasing in size.

11. **(2)** *Comprehension/Economics.* The examples of what each worker does show that the production process was broken down into many simple steps. Choice (1) is incorrect, since production at home is not mentioned. Nothing is said about machines, so choice (3) cannot be right. Choice (4) is contradicted by the passage, which indicates that the process became faster and more efficient. Choice (5) is also incorrect, since it was the individual steps of the process that were simplified and not the overall process.

12. **(2)** *Analysis/Economics.* The workers that Smith describes are doing less complicated tasks than earlier pinmakers, each of whom had performed the entire process. Therefore choices (1) and (3) are incorrect. Since the new process just involves dividing old skills among many workers, and does not involve any new steps or skills, choice (4) is wrong. Although simplified, the job is not automatic, so choice (5) is also incorrect.

13. **(5)** *Analysis/Economics.* The author says that with the new process many more pins can be produced in much less time. It therefore makes sense that pins would become more plentiful and cheaper. Choices (3) and (4) are therefore wrong. Choice (2) is unlikely: If more pins can be made and sold, pinmaking should become more, not less, profitable. Choice (1) is not supported by anything in the passage.

14. **(2)** *Application/Economics.* As people switched from hunting to farming, the standard of living rose because more goods could be produced. It follows that a modern nation that wants to improve its standard of living would have to increase its production. Although farming was a more productive way of obtaining food than hunting, this does not mean that <u>modern</u> nations could improve their standard of living by promoting farming, as in choice (1). Choices (3), (4), and (5) are unlikely in themselves to lead to a better standard of living.

15. **(3)** *Comprehension/Economics.* The passage describes an ongoing shift in the job market from blue-collar to service jobs. The ideas in choices (1) and (2) appear in the passage but as details or background information. Choices (4) and (5) are not covered in the passage.

16. **(3)** *Application/Economics.* The passage states that the job market in the years to come will be dominated by well-trained professional, managerial, and technical workers. Thus it can be concluded that education will be an important asset for job seekers. Although the information says unemployment decreased, it does not say that unemployment is being eliminated or that jobs will be easy to find, contrary to choice (1). Choice (2) contradicts the government statistics about service jobs. The advice in choices (4) and (5) is not supported by the information.

17. **(2)** *Analysis/Economics.* The passage says that some observers believe the decline in manufacturing jobs means the economy is in trouble but goes on to show why others disagree. Thus, the statement in choice (2) is an opinion rather than a fact. Choices (1), (3), and (4) are facts about employment trends. Choice (5) is a fact about job requirements.

18. **(2)** *Evaluation/Economics.* There are over 62 million more service jobs than there are high-tech jobs. Furthermore, a much higher percentage of service jobs as opposed to high-tech jobs are reported to be low paying (41.9 percent versus 12.4 percent). Therefore, it can be concluded that there are many more low-paying service jobs than there are low-paying high-tech jobs. Choices (1), (3), and (4) cannot be supported without further information. Choice (5) is contradicted by the graphs.

19. **(3)** *Analysis/Economics.* Sales were low. Manufacturers hoped that the new short skirts would make women feel that their clothes were "old-fashioned" and had to be replaced. If this happened, sales would rise. Choice (1) is directly contradicted. Choice (2) is not supported. The passage mentions that manufacturers were taking the risk that the short skirts wouldn't sell, so choice (4) can't be correct. Nothing is said about being different from the competition, as in choice (5).

20. **(3)** *Analysis/Economics.* Manufacturers introduced short skirts hoping to influence consumer tastes. But they also knew there was a chance women wouldn't buy these short skirts. Therefore the passage supports the statement in choice (3). The text does not support the relationship between consumers and manufacturers expressed in the other choices.

21. **(3)** *Comprehension/Economics.* The total row ("all renter households") at the bottom shows that 32.9 percent, or close to one-third, of all renter households paid more than 40 percent of their income in rent. Therefore choice (2) is wrong. Choice (1) is also wrong since the table shows that only 228,000 of 1,900,000 households had an income of $35,000 or more. Choice (4) cannot be supported by the table because the table does not report about rents that equal 100 percent of income. (Furthermore, only households in the lowest income bracket spent more than 40 percent of their income on rent.) As for choice (5), the table shows that 45.6 percent of the people in this bracket spent <u>more</u> than 25 percent of their income on rent; therefore, only 54.4 percent spent less than 25 percent.

22. **(2)** *Evaluation/Economics.* Since most people either rent or buy their housing, the data in the table, together with data on home owners, would give a reasonably full picture about portions of income spent on housing in New York City.

23. **(2)** *Evaluation/Economics.* In the lower income brackets high percentages of households spent more than 40 percent of their income on housing. In the highest income brackets, few households spent even as much as 25 percent of their income on housing. No choice other than (2) can be supported on the basis of the table alone.

24. **(2)** *Application/Economics.* The table shows that the vast majority of households in New York City that earned less than $10,000 paid more than 40 percent of their income in rent. This would suggest a need for more affordable housing. None of the other recommendations are directly suggested by the data.

25. **(3)** *Comprehension/Economics.* The information mentions that retail store cards and gas company cards are the easiest to obtain. The statements in the other choices are all contradicted in the information.

26. **(3)** *Application/Economics.* Since the consumer wants to be able to spread payments out, she cannot use a T&E card, as in choice (5); T&E card bills have to be paid off immediately. A retail card

while allowing payments to be spread out, would involve high interest payments. Therefore, choice (1) can be ruled out. The consumer's needs would best be met by a bank card with low interest rates. Choices (2) and (4) do not ensure low interest rates.

27. **(4)** *Application/Economics.* Travel and entertainment cards have no spending limits but require that charges be paid on receipt of the monthly bill. They would, therefore, be most appropriate for the individual described in choice (4). The individuals in the others choices have credit needs that would best be met by one of the other kinds of credit cards discussed in the information.

28. **(2)** *Evaluation/Economics.* The information indicates that some kinds of cards are easier to obtain than others. As this implies, however, all cards have to be applied for, and applications are in no case automatically granted.

29. **(4)** *Comprehension/Economics.* The passage indicates that more than half the charges were applied to bank cards.

30. **(4)** *Analysis/Economics.* There are no annual fees for retail store and gas company cards, and interest is charged on only outstanding balances. By using those kinds of cards and paying her monthly bills in full, Edna would never spend more than the cost of her purchases. If she used bank or T&E cards—as in choices (1), (2), (3), and (5)—she would have to pay at least the annual fees in addition to charges for purchases.

Political Science Items

1. **(1)** *Application/Political Science.* You are being asked how long you have held an opinion. You are not being asked how strong it is, how active it is or how closely it affects you. Nor is the pollster directly measuring how divided the voters are.

2. **(4)** *Application/Political Science.* Deep involvement shows how much you identify with or are affected by an issue, so salience is the appropriate answer. The question is getting at personal identification and involvement, so intensity, although related, is not correct.

3. **(5)** *Application/Political Science.* The extent to which voters as a whole agree about an issue, as in this case, is a measure of polarization.

4. **(3)** *Application/Political Science.* Establishing a military alliance with other free world countries is an application of the containment policy because it would put the United States in a better position to resist Soviet demands and strengthen the other nations in the alliance. Cutting back on foreign aid or taking a less active role in foreign affairs, choices (1) and (5), would go against the containment policy. Negotiating with the Soviet Union, choice (2), is also not the best choice, since containment focuses on resisting Soviet demands rather than negotiating about them. Increasing exports, in choice (4), is an economic issue unrelated to containment.

5. **(4)** *Analysis/Political Science.* Whether special-interest groups have too big a say and whether lobbyists have had a harmful effect on the political system are more matters of opinion than fact. The statements in the other choices are facts and are presented as such in the information.

6. **(3)** *Evaluation/Political Science.* The fact that lobbyists are experts on certain issues and can share their expertise with congresspeople would be an argument in favor of lobbyists. The statements in all the choices would be more appropriate for making an argument <u>against</u> lobbyists.

7. **(1)** *Evaluation/Political Science.* Personal and corporate income taxes account for 54 percent of the total income. As corporate taxes alone by no means account for most of the government's income, choice (4) is incorrect. Choices (2), (3), and (5) all involve information that is not covered in the graph.

8. **(3)** *Analysis/Political Science.* The graphs show that one-third of all economic aid and nearly two-thirds of all military aid go to countries in the Middle East. From this it can be concluded that the United States regards the Middle East as an area of considerable importance. Choice (1) is not supported, especially since far more is spent on economic aid than military aid. Choice (2) cannot be supported by only these graphs. Choices (4) and (5) are if anything, contradicted in view of the low level of military aid to Latin America and the Caribbean and the low level of economic aid to Europe.

9. **(2)** *Comprehension/Political Science.* Latin America and the Caribbean receive 16 percent of the total $7,580 billion given in economic aid but only 4.4 percent of the smaller total of $4,949 billion

given in military aid. Therefore, contrary to choice (2), Latin America and the Caribbean receive more in economic aid than in military aid. All the other choices are supported by information in the graphs.

10. **(2)** *Comprehension/Political Science.* The speaker says that with a position high in government, it is possible to line up "big buck deals." The tone and meaning of the words "big buck deals" suggests corruption. Some people in high positions in government arrange contracts with private manufacturers. Sometimes, in order to gain the contracts, private companies bribe government officials. That could be a "big buck deal" for the official. Choice (1) is not right because "big buck deals" does not mean "salary." Choices (3), (4), and (5) are not addressed by the cartoon.

11. **(2)** *Evaluation/Political Science.* Since categorical grants allow the federal government to specify how money will be used, approve plans, and supervise projects, they give the government significant control over the money and its use. Revenue-sharing grants, in contrast, give the main control to the states. Therefore, choice (2) is correct, and choice (5) must be wrong. The statements in choices (1), (3), and (4) cannot be supported by the information.

12. **(3)** *Comprehension/Political Science.* In council-manager governments, there is a city manager appointed by the city council; in mayor-council governments, there is no city manager. Choice (1) is unlikely and like choices (2) and (5) is not supported. Choice (4) is contradicted by the chart, which shows that both forms of city government have a mayor.

13. **(4)** *Analysis/Political Science.* The chart shows that in the council-manager form of government, the city manager, who is in charge of administering the city departments, is appointed by the council rather than elected by voters. In the mayor-council form of government, departments are administered by the mayor, who is elected. In this sense, then, voters have less power in cities with council-manager governments because they do not elect the person who administers. The statements in choices (1), (2), and (5) are not relevant to explaining a difference in voter power. Choice (3) focuses on similarities between the two forms of government and does not explain differences in voter power.

14. **(3)** *Analysis/Political Science.* Harriman says the U.S. and USSR must settle areas in which agreement is possible to preserve peace. He could not have believed that war is inevitable or desirable, as in choices (1) and (5), since he speaks of trying to live together in peace. He says that there is no possibility of the U.S. and the USSR compromising on ideology, so he must not believe that the countries' ideologies are similar, as in choice (2), or that the U.S. should adopt the Soviet system, as in choice (4).

15. **(5)** *Application/Political Science.* A mutual arms reduction agreement is an example of settling issues in a nonideological area and working toward peace. The actions in the other choices do not involve working together; they would probably cause further hostility between the U.S. and USSR.

16. **(4)** *Comprehension/Political Science.* Uncle Sam, like Snow White's stepmother, is surprised not to see his own face looking back from the mirror, when he asks, "Who's the most influential...?" Thus it can be concluded that the United States no longer has the influence in the United Nations that it once had.

17. **(4)** *Comprehension/Political Science.* Several of the treaties shown are labeled "mutual defense treaties." This indicates that the purpose of the treaties must be military.

18. **(1)** *Evaluation/Political Science.* World War II ended in 1945, and all the treaties shown have dates in the late forties or early fifties. These treaties were therefore signed in the cold war period. Choice (2) is contradicted, since some of the treaties involve only the United States and one other country. Choice (5) is also contradicted, since none of the treaties involves countries in Africa. There is nothing in the map to support choice (3) or choice (4).

19. **(4)** *Application/Political Science.* The American government pursued an isolationist policy by keeping out of international organizations and affairs.

20. **(1)** *Application/Political Science.* Great Britain had long-term control in India for purposes of Britain's own prestige, defense, and economic gain.

21. **(5)** *Application/Political Science.* Egypt has participated in international affairs but has not sided with either of the two superpowers.

22. **(2)** *Application/Political Science.* Ties to other nations through treaties and world and regional organizations illustrate a U.S. foreign policy of internationalism.

23. **(3)** *Application/Political Science.* Only the individual described in choice (3) meets the age, citizenship, and residency qualifications for election to the Senate from California.

24. **(3)** *Application/Political Science.* In ruling that a law violates the First Amendment, the Supreme Court is exercising the judiciary's power to determine whether laws and acts are in keeping with the Constitution. None of the other choices describe testing a law or executive act for constitutionality.

25. **(1)** *Analysis/Political Science.* As the power to levy and collect taxes is a shared power, it follows that individuals will pay taxes to both the federal and the state governments. No rationale for the other statements can be found in the diagram.

26. **(2)** *Comprehension/Political Science.* Since regulation of foreign commerce is a power that is given only to the federal government, states may not sign trade agreements with foreign countries. Choices (1) and (3) involve uses of powers given only to state governments. Choices (4) and (5) involve uses of shared power.

27. **(4)** *Application/Political Science.* The granting of pardons to criminals is the only function that is related to administration of justice. The other functions are all executive or quasi-legislative.

28. **(5)** *Comprehension/Political Science.* The passage discusses and gives examples of how negative freedom and positive freedom are both important parts of our political heritage. Choice (1) cannot be right, since freedoms are largely expressed through laws. Choice (2) is contradicted by the fact that the United States emphasizes both negative and positive freedom. Negative freedom is an older idea than positive freedom, contrary to choice (3). The passage implies that the two freedoms are equally important, contrary to choice (4).

29. **(4)** *Application/Political Science.* The right to petition government is a "freedom to." Petitioning gives citizens a way to act. Therefore it is a positive freedom. All the other choices are examples of negative freedom or of how government is prevented from taking certain actions.

30. **(1)** *Application/Political Science.* Preventing judges from setting excessive bails and fines is a restriction on the actions of government officials. It is therefore an example of "freedom from." All the other choices are examples of positive freedom: Before slaves became citizens, they were prevented from a range of actions; the granting of citizenship, in choice (2), removed these obstacles. Choices (3)–(5) all involve extensions of voting rights.

Behavioral Science Items

1. **(1)** *Evaluation/Behavioral Science.* A comparison of the percentages for the different regions shows that the Northeast has the lowest percent of firearms usage in murder, assault, and robbery. Since firearms usage rates are highest for the South, choice (2) is wrong. Choice (3) is contradicted by the table, which shows that usage is higher in robberies than in assaults. The table does not provide the information needed to support choices (4) or (5).

2. **(3)** *Evaluation/Behavioral Science.* Since taboo behaviors are ones that customs strongly discourage, they are less likely to occur than behaviors that are not taboo. Choices (1) and (2) are contradicted by the passage. Choices (4) and (5) are not supported by anything in the passage.

3. **(3)** *Analysis/Behavioral Science.* The Polynesian "taboo" is essentially a prohibition based on fear of the supernatural rather than on law. The social science term describes a prohibition based on custom rather than law. Choice (1) is wrong: incest is only one example of a taboo. Although the supernatural, in choice (2), is part of the original Polynesian concept, it is not part of what social scientists mean by "taboo." Choice (4) is wrong because social science—especially its use of "taboo"—is not centuries old. The passage does not support the claim in choice (5).

4. **(2)** *Application/Behavioral Science.* The response emphasizes the opinions of other people as the basis for determining what is right and wrong.

5. **(5)** *Application/Behavioral Science.* The response is based on the person's own belief that human life is the most important value.

6. **(1)** *Application/Behavioral Science.* The response is centered on the fact that the authorities punish stealing.

7. **(3)** *Application/Behavioral Science.* The response emphasizes the importance of obeying the law.

8. **(4)** *Application/Behavioral Science.* The problem is stated by the sign the man is holding: In today's "escalator education" schools, "everybody passes." Students easily reach the top, only to tumble down because they lack skills. Thus the problem that this cartoonist sees could best be addressed by establishing tougher standards in schools.

9. **(2)** *Comprehension/Behavioral Science.* The America-Iran example illustrates how different cultures have quite different ideas about the personality differences between men and women. The ideas in choices (1) and (5) are not discussed. Choice (3) is part of the example, not the main idea. The statement in choice (4) is too general, and makes much too strong a statement.

10. **(2)** *Evaluation/Behavioral Science.* Any culture encourages the behavior that fits its expectations about how men and women should behave. Therefore, it is likely that personality differences between men and women are influenced by cultural factors. Choices (1), (4) and (5) as hypotheses are contradicted by the information. There is nothing in the passage about choice (3).

11. **(4)** *Analysis/Behavioral Science.* The poverty rate is highest for those under 15 years of age. This suggests there is an urgent need to develop more income-earning opportunities for parents of these children, who are probably included in the 15–24 group—with the second highest poverty rate—and the 25–44 group.

12. **(4)** *Evaluation/Behavioral Science.* The graph shows that there are many more elderly women than elderly men in Illinois. Therefore we can reasonably conclude that the life expectancy is greater for women than for men. As no information is given on other states, choices (1) and (2) can't be supported. The graph seems to indicate an increase in life expectancy over the period, contrary to choice (3). Nothing is said about years worked, as in choice (5).

13. **(1)** *Evaluation/Behavioral Science.* At the time pitchers were trying to win long-term contracts, their performance improved. Once they won their contracts, however, their performance dropped off. This supports the idea that motivation—in this case to win a contract—has a positive effect on performance and the lack of motivation has a negative effect. Choices (2), (4), and (5) are all contradicted by the fact that performance improved and then worsened. Choice (3) does not make sense, since the changes in performance seemed to follow a pattern.

14. **(3)** *Evaluation/Behavioral Science.* The table shows that enrollments expanded very slowly from 1932 to 1958, but then jumped in the 1960s and 1970s. This sudden jump supports the statement in choice (3). None of the other choices can be supported on the basis of the information in the table.

15. **(3)** *Analysis/Behavioral Science.* If learning to delay gratification is a necessary step in achieving self-control, then it follows that someone who has self-control is able to delay gratification. The other statements do not follow from the information, and the statement in choice (4) is contradicted by it.

16. **(3)** *Application/Behavioral Science.* Working overtime to save money for school requires giving up time and pleasures for the sake of a long-term goal. The situation in choice (1) is the opposite of delayed gratification—putting pleasure before work. The situations in choices (2), (4), and (5) don't involve postponing gratification for later reward.

17. **(2)** *Comprehension/Behavioral Science.* Psychologists wanted to see whether the feeling of being "just a face in the crowd" would lead people to do things they presumably wouldn't approve of, like vandalize a car. New York City and the California town were chosen, not because they were on the East and West Coasts, as in choice (3), but because one was an "anonymous" environment and the other wasn't.

18. **(5)** *Analysis/Behavioral Science.* New York, but not California had the anonymous environment. And well-dressed adults are people who would seem likely to disapprove of vandalism. Therefore, the fact that the car was vandalized in New York, but not California and the fact that well-dressed adults vandalized the car both support the hypothesis. Choices (3) and (4) suggest that the hypothesis was contradicted by the findings. The facts in choices (1) and (2) do not disprove the hypothesis; they support it.

19. **(1)** *Evaluation/Behavioral Science.* The statement in choice (1) is supported by the study's finding that people in a city behaved differently from people in a small

town when the opportunity to vandalize arose. Choice (2) may be true, but the experiment addresses only the negative side of anonymity. The fact that the car in California wasn't vandalized isn't enough evidence to support the conclusion that there's no crime in small towns, as in choice (3). Choice (4) involves a value judgment. Choice (5) can't be supported by the experiment, which didn't try to look at crimes other than vandalism.

20. **(3)** *Application/Behavioral Science.* The experiment in choice (3) looks at two different towns. It doesn't compare a town with a more anonymous environment. Therefore, this experiment wouldn't reveal anything about whether the hypothesis is right or wrong. All the other experiments listed in some way compare people's actions in a large city and in a small town.

21. **(3)** *Comprehension/Behavioral Science.* By the end of the period shown, women made up a higher percentage of the total number of lawyers, bank officials and finance managers, mechanics, assembly workers, bus drivers, and police. These were all traditionally male professions. Choice (1) is incorrect, since most of the jobs shown had either a significantly higher percentage of male workers or a significantly higher percentage of female workers. Choice (2) is wrong, since the percentage of women in the two traditionally female jobs shown—teaching and secretarial work—actually rose slightly. For this same reason, choice (4) is unlikely. Choice (5) is wrong, since women are not shown as coming to represent a majority of the workers in the traditionally male fields.

22. **(2)** *Comprehension/Behavioral Science.* People go through initiation rites when they are about to take on new roles. The rites symbolize entry into a new phase in life.

23. **(3)** *Application/Behavioral Science.* An engagement party, a wedding, a graduation ceremony, and a retirement party all mark the beginning of a new phase in an individual's life. A Thanksgiving dinner, in contrast, marks a holiday that is celebrated each year.

24. **(2)** *Comprehension/Behavioral Science.* Pullman said he didn't want his workers to live in the unhealthy conditions characteristic of a big city environment. Nothing in the passage supports the motives proposed in the other choices.

25. **(2)** *Analysis/Behavioral Science.* Pullman wanted the town to be orderly and beautiful for his workers. He also wanted to make a profit for his company, through workers buying at his stores and renting his houses. Choices (1) and (4) are incorrect, since Pullman wasn't building the town only for the sake of his workers. The statement in choice (3) was expressed by Richard Ely, not by George Pullman. Contrary to choice (5), Pullman believed big cities were unhealthy for workers.

26. **(2)** *Analysis/Behavioral Science.* Ely described the town as a situation where workers would be well-treated but would be "underlings," under the thumbs of the authorities, that is, of their company. Ely praised the beauty and healthfulness of the town, so choice (1) is incorrect. Ely called the town "un-American" because of the situation of the workers, not for the reason mentioned in choice (3). The quote from Ely contains nothing to support choices (4) or (5).

27. **(4)** *Analysis/Behavioral Science.* The statement in choice (4) is an opinion, as indicated by the fact that George Pullman probably would have agreed with it whereas Richard Ely probably would have disagreed. The statements in the other choices are given as facts; no one could disagree with them.

28. **(4)** *Comprehension/Behavioral Science.* The passage describes the purpose and process of desensitization. Although the other choices are stated or implied in the passage, they are just details that support the main theme of the passage.

29. **(4)** *Analysis/Behavioral Science.* Desensitization gets people to respond in calm ways to situations that once made them anxious. Therefore the method must assume that people can learn to change their response to situations. Since the method doesn't involve talk or expectations, choices (1) and (5) cannot be correct. Since the method tries to get people over their anxiety, choices (2) and (3) cannot be correct.

30. **(5)** *Application/Behavioral Science.* Choice (5) alone involves counterconditioning: relaxing in an anxiety-producing situation. Since being in a plane on the ground is less anxiety producing than being in the air, the person first practices relaxing in this situation.

1. **(3)** *Application/Behavioral Science.* The sculptor rejects society's goal of financial success. But she accepts the means of hard work and does not break society's rules.
2. **(4)** *Application/Behavioral Science.* The politician pursues the goal of financial success. But he apparently does so less through hard work than through other—even illegal—means.
3. **(5)** *Application/Behavioral Science.* The commune members have rejected both the goals and means of their society. They emphasize the goal of spiritual growth rather than financial success, and they do only the amount of work needed to survive.
4. **(1)** *Application/Behavioral Science.* In his work and in his home life, the surgeon shows that he has pursued society's goals according to the accepted means.
5. **(4)** *Application/Behavioral Science.* The drug dealer has pursued and achieved the goal of economic success but has not done so through means that the society accepts.
6. **(1)** *Analysis/Economics.* If a country's economy is improving, it is likely that more businesses will be starting up and fewer will be failing. The other choices describe economies that are either not improving or failing.
7. **(1)** *Comprehension/Political Science.* Elections depend on citizens voting, and ultimately, Americans' freedom depends on elections. If citizens don't vote, the cartoon is saying, Americans will end up on "Freedom's Skid Row." There is no clear chain of events between not voting and the situations mentioned in choices (2)–(4). Choice (5) is contrary to the message of the cartoon.
8. **(4)** *Comprehension/History.* The cartoon shows President Roosevelt marching through the Caribbean, armed with a big stick and a fleet of ships with names like "Debt Collector" and "The Sheriff." These symbols indicate that President Roosevelt's "Big Stick" policy had the United States playing the role of a policeman in the Caribbean. Choices (1) and (5) are contradicted by the cartoon. There is nothing in the cartoon to support choice (2) or choice (3), which deal with trade and economic aid.
9. **(4)** *Evaluation/History.* President Roosevelt is shown as a giant with a giant stick, far larger than the Caribbean countries themselves. This suggests that the cartoonist saw Roosevelt's policy as somewhat exaggerated given the circumstances. None of the other choices can explain Roosevelt's giant size.
10. **(5)** *Analysis/Geography.* Since tundra regions are in the Arctic beyond the point at which trees can grow, it follows that they do not have the appropriate conditions to support agriculture. Choices (1) and (2) are not likely since tundra occurs in a limited area. Its location and characteristics make choice (3) unlikely. Nothing is said to support choice (4).
11. **(2)** *Analysis/History.* Choice (2) is the only conclusion that can be drawn. According to the graph, from 1900–1930 the largest group of immigrants were laborers who would not be college educated. The only group with college education would be "Professional, technical, and like." Choice (1) is incorrect because at the turn of the 20th century (1900), most workers were laborers. The occupation of skilled workers could be "craftsmen, foremast, operatives, and like." Choice (3) is also wrong because in 1940 the largest group of immigrants were the professionals and technicians. There was a decline in office workers (clerical, sales, and like) from 1960–1977, so choice (4) is wrong. Choice (5) is eliminated since information about ethnicity is not provided, and the occupations are indeed diverse.
12. **(5)** *Evaluation/Economics.* Distribution is most unequal in Mexico, where the wealthiest hold nearly half of the country's income—more than in the other two countries. So choice (5) is right and choices (1), (3), and (4) are wrong. Choice (2) is wrong because the poorest in East Germany have more of their country's wealth than in the United States.
13. **(2)** *Analysis/Economics.* The table shows that the poorest in East Germany have a larger share of their country's income than in the United States. Therefore, choice (1) is wrong. However, without knowing the total income in each case, it is impossible to make any comparisons. The chart <u>defines</u> the poorest as 10 percent of the population, so choice (3) is wrong. The total population and location of the two countries has no bearing on the comparison between them, as suggested by choices (4) and (5).

14. **(1)** *Analysis/History.* By raising the price of foreign manufactured goods, the tariff encouraged, or even forced, consumers to buy domestic manufactured goods. Benefiting from and supporting the tariff were Northern manufacturers. Consumers, Southern farmers, and foreign countries were, if anything, hurt by the tariff and therefore were unlikely to support it.

15. **(1)** *Evaluation/Geography.* The map shows that in January, southern states receive from 200 to 350 calories per square centimeter per day of solar energy whereas northern states received 150 to 250. Choice (2) is contradicted by the map. Choices (3) and (4) cannot be supported on the basis of the map. Choice (5) cannot be correct, since the map shows the importance of location.

16. **(2)** *Comprehension/Geography.* The map shows that on days of average cloudiness the states of the Pacific Northwest receive 100 calories per square centimeter per day of solar energy. The other regions mentioned are all shown as receiving greater amounts of solar energy.

17. **(2)** *Comprehension/Political Science.* The information focuses on the differences between the party column ballot and the office bloc ballot. None of the topics mentioned in the other choices is specifically discussed.

18. **(3)** *Application/Political Science.* The information explains that by grouping candidates from a party together, the party column ballot encourages voters to vote straight tickets. It does not say that such ballots increase voter turnout. If people vote for a presidential candidate, the party column ballot encourages them to vote for other candidates of the president's party as well. Such candidates would prefer a party column ballot.

19. **(5)** *Application/Political Science.* An office bloc ballot encourages voters to split their tickets. It could therefore encourage voters to choose a governor from one party but other candidates from other parties. Nothing in the information suggests that the situations described in the other choices would result from the use of an office bloc ballot.

20. **(4)** *Analysis/Behavioral Science.* The psychologists are arguing that older people have characteristics and capacities that would make them good workers. Therefore, choice (4) is supported and choice (5) can be ruled out. The recommendations in choices (1), (2), and (3) do not follow from the view the psychologists are arguing.

21. **(3)** *Comprehension/Economics.* The cartoon shows a worker menaced by a machine labeled automation and threatening to "strike" back. There is no evidence of injury, as in choice (2). The ground is being eaten away from under the worker. The worker thinks his job is being undermined by technology. Choice (1) is wrong because the worker's fear is of the consequences of mechanization, not of machines, themselves. Choice (4) is wrong since the worker seems to think that to strike (as a job action, or physically) is threatening. Choice (5) is wrong because the worker is all too aware of technological progress that threatens his job.

22. **(5)** *Evaluation/Economics.* Clearly the worker's attempt to fight automation is not realistic. Automation is too powerful a force; it results in increases of unemployment. Choices (1), (2), and (3) are opinions that have little to do with the issue the cartoon addresses. Choice (4) is contradicted by the cartoon.

23. **(2)** *Analysis/Economics.* Choices (1), (3), (4) and (5) are all efforts to make U.S. products more competitive. Because of labor unions, rising inflation, and the high cost of living, companies could not lower wages. Instead, they have not given wage increases. Using robots and automated machines allows businesses to increase productivity with fewer workers, thus, cutting labor costs but also increasing unemployment. In recent years, there has been a lot of cooperation between U.S. (Ford and General Motors) and Japanese auto makers (Toyota, Nissan, and Mitsubishi).

24. **(1)** *Application/Geography.* In choice (1), economic activities are influenced by the island environment. Choices (2)–(4) are examples of the other part of the interaction, that is, of humans' effect on the environment. Choice (5) does not directly involve the environment: It shows humans influenced by technology that they themselves develop.

25. **(1)** *Comprehension/History.* The passage is a general discussion of the ways in which bosses abused their political power for their own profit and how they were able to stay in power despite those abuses.

26. **(2)** *Analysis/History.* Bosses got lots of votes from immigrants and other urban poor who, having no welfare agencies to

turn to in times of trouble, turned to the bosses and remained loyal to them on election day. Once national and state welfare programs were created, people didn't need to turn to the bosses for help. In this way, the bosses lost much of their support. Choices (4) and (5) would, if anything, tend to give the bosses more support. There is nothing in the passage to indicate the relevance of choices (1) and (3).

27. **(2)** *Evaluation/History.* Bosses used the democratic system to stay in power. They found supporters who would, for the wrong reasons, keep voting them in. Thus, under bosses, democracy existed but in a corrupted form. Choice (1) is wrong, since citizens did vote. Choices (3), (4), and (5) are wrong, since bosses misused the democratic system and were virtually assured of reelection.

28. **(3)** *Analysis/History.* Based on the passage, bosses saw political office mainly as an opportunity to make large sums of money. The arrival of immigrants, choice (1), was a means by which bosses stayed in power, and not their reason for staying in power. Nothing is said about Senate seats, as in choice (2). Although bosses may have helped people, as in choice (4), this wasn't their main goal. Bosses' procedures for awarding contracts suggest that ensuring the wise growth of the cities, choice (5), was also not their main goal.

29. **(3)** *Evaluation/History.* The graph shows that in periods of economic recessions, indicated by shading, the unemployment rate tends to go up. Choice (1) is incorrect, since during wars unemployment tends to go down. Choice (2) cannot be correct: If presidential elections years were associated with drops in unemployment, the chart would show drops at regular four-year intervals, and it does not. Choice (4) cannot be supported, especially since there is not steady rise in unemployment. Choice (5) cannot be supported, since figures for other countries are not given.

30. **(5)** *Application/Geography.* The passage says that each zone observes a time that is one hour earlier than the zone to its east. Denver is two time zones west of Philadelphia. Two zones will make the time two hours earlier in Denver than in Philadelphia.

31. **(5)** *Application/Political Science.* According to the seniority system, the committee chairperson will be the person from the majority party who has been on that committee the longest. In the example given, the Democrats are the House majority party.

32. **(1)** *Analysis/Political Science.* Since length of service on the committee is the basis for choosing the chairperson, the committee chairpeople are generally highly experienced. Choices (2) and (5) are not supported by the information. Choice (3) is specifically contradicted. Choice (4) is unlikely, since the chairpeople, far from being new to the committee, have been on it for a long time.

Full-Length Practice Test

1. **(5)** *Evaluation/History.* The graph reports changes in levels of immigration to the United States. Immigration laws and economic and political conditions at home and abroad, as in choices (1)–(4), would all significantly affect how many people come to the United States. Movements of people within the United States, in choice (5), would be much less likely to have a direct effect on immigration levels.

2. **(1)** *Evaluation/History.* The beginning of the century had the highest levels of immigration. It is therefore very unlikely that the United States had a restrictive immigration policy at the beginning of the century. The drop in number of immigrants in the 1920s and 1930s supports choices (2) and (3). The rise in the late 1940s supports choice (4), while the rise in the 1960s and 1970s supports choice (5).

3. **(3)** *Evaluation/Economics.* Matters related to international trade are part of economics. Even though there may be economic aspects to them, the other questions would be addressed by other social scientists.

4. **(2)** *Evaluation/Behavioral Science.* Since aggression is a response to frustration, we can say that frustration can lead to aggression. The information does not suggest that aggression can lead to frustration, as in choice (3), or that displacement can lead to aggression, as in choice (1). The claims in choices (4) and (5) are neither made nor implied in the information.

5. **(4)** *Analysis/Behavioral Science.* Displacement involves expressing one's frustration aggressively with less risk. Instead of confronting the person causing our frustrations, we take out our feelings on someone else who is safe or close to us such as a spouse, friend or relative. Choices (2) and (5) are incorrect because they do not involve aggressive behavior toward another person. Choice (3) is incorrect because an employee's boss would not be considered a "safe" target. Choice (1) is also incorrect; it is not a hypothesis because we do not know why the mother slapped her daughter. It could have been to punish or set an example for the child but not because the mother was feeling frustrated.

6. **(1)** *Application/Behavioral Science.* The salesperson can't vent his frustration on his customers, the proper target, as by doing so he might jeopardize his job, and so he directs it instead at his secretary. The individuals in choices (2), (3), and (5) feel frustrated but are not acting in an aggressive way toward anyone. The individual in choice (4) acts in an aggressive way, but no displacement is involved: He yells at his boss, who made him angry, even though that yelling is risky.

7. **(4)** *Evaluation/Geography.* How extensive a country's transportation system is will very directly affect whether people stay near home or travel farther afield to carry on routine activities. None of the other factors can have a direct effect on the amount of activity space typical in a country.

8. **(4)** *Comprehension/Geography.* The second figure shows that 65 million years ago, North America had fully broken away from Africa but was still partially attached to Eurasia. All the other statements are supported by the figures.

9. **(3)** *Analysis/Geography.* The figures show that the Atlantic Ocean was created when the "super-continent" broke up. It widened as the continents drifted. The other choices are contradicted by the figures.

10. **(2)** *Comprehension/Economics.* There are two major types of money, currency and demand deposits. Currency accounts for less than one-third of all money. Therefore, most of the money used is in the form of demand deposits, or checks, and checking account holders are the largest issuers of money. This logic makes all the choices but (2) wrong.

11. **(4)** *Evaluation/History.* The statement in choice (4) emphasizes the powers of the states and the fact that the states came before and created the federal government, which includes Congress. It could therefore be used to support the states' rights position. Choice (5) is irrelevant to the states' rights position. Choices (1), (2), and (3) could be used to argue against the position.

12. **(2)** *Analysis/Economics.* Higher crop yields would mean more food for the populations. Choice (1) is not correct because a change in agricultural production would not have a direct effect on manufacturing. Choice (4) is, if anything, contradicted, since higher yields could mean increased agricultural exports. Choice (5) is unlikely, since the difference was that the new grains produced higher yields, not that they could be grown in new environments. There is nothing to support choice (3).

13. **(4)** *Comprehension/Behavioral Science.* The graph deals with people's expectations regarding the economic situation in their countries. It shows that in every case the percentage of people who thought there would be economic difficulty increased from 1977 to 1980. Choice (2) is contradicted. Choices (1), (3), and (5) do not relate to the information in the graph.

14. **(2)** *Analysis/Behavioral Science.* A shortage of jobs makes workers more concerned with holding on to their jobs than with other issues related to their jobs. It therefore makes sense that when the economy is doing well, and jobs are consequently more plentiful, workers will become more interested in other issues like job satisfaction. There is nothing to indicate that the government's role in the economy will have an effect, as in choice (1). Choices (3), (4), and (5) are likely to threaten the individual's job or to make jobs in general more scarce. Therefore these choices can all be ruled out.

15. **(1)** *Application/Political Science.* The example concerns an event on a United States waterway.

16. **(2)** *Application/Political Science.* John Jones is seeking to protect his reputation from Sam Smith's slander. Laws governing the relationships between individuals are therefore involved.

17. **(5)** *Application/Political Science.* In the example, the Supreme Court established law by interpreting the Constitution.

18. **(4)** *Application/Political Science.* Federal administrators on the Federal Trade Commission have produced a regulation; this regulation becomes part of administrative law.

19. **(2)** *Analysis/History* You can conclude that Cuba was turning to communism because after gaining power, Fidel established a close relationship with the Soviet Union and practiced Marxism, the economic theory which predicts the eventual collapse of capitalism and its replacement with socialism and then communism. The passage does not mention anything about U.S. influence throughout the Caribbean nor Cuban exiles' desire to return home [choices (1) and (3)]. The invasion failed because of Fidel's popular support, so choice (4) is incorrect. Kennedy was not bound by the policies and plans of previous administrations as suggested in choice (5).

20. **(1)** *Analysis/History.* The CIA and the exiles believed that an invasion would set off an uprising and that a small group of men could in this way overthrow Castro's government. The invasion proved these assumptions wrong. The explanations in choices (2)–(5) cannot be supported by the information given.

21. **(3)** *Evaluation/History.* The president did not regret the decision to send the mission to Cuba, a Communist country with ties to Russia, and he warned Russia of the United States intention to protect the hemisphere against "external aggression." Therefore, it can be concluded that Kennedy wanted to resist Communist penetration of the hemisphere, as in choice (3). Choice (1) is wrong, since the passage says Castro had close relations with Russia. Choice (2) simply cannot be supported on the basis of the information given and in fact seems unlikely. Choices (4) and (5) are contradicted by information in the passage.

22. **(4)** *Application/History.* Both the Cuban and the Nicaraguan cases involve the U.S. government giving some form of support to rebels seeking to oust a Marxist regime from a Western Hemisphere country. Choice (1) is wrong since the project had a very different purpose, did not take place in Latin America, and involved the use of airpower. Choice (2) is incorrect since U.S. soldiers were directly involved and the aim was not to overthrow a Communist regime but rather to collect debts. Choice (3) is wrong because it involved U.S. volunteers in Europe fighting in support of a leftist government. Choice (5) is wrong since American troops were directly involved and since the action had nothing to do with overthrowing a government.

23. **(2)** *Analysis/Economics.* Choices (1) and (3) are opinions expressed by "harder" and "more ambitious." There is no information about overtime in the chart, so choice (5) is incorrect. The chart compares the percentage of earnings between men and women who are working; the number of women who are unemployed and are at home is not relevant. Also, "forced" makes choice (4) an opinion. Choice (2) is the correct answer. Throughout history, women have been discriminated against in the work force by not receiving equal pay for equal work, not having the same opportunities for promotions, and not having access to high positions as men have had.

24. **(5)** *Analysis/Economics.* The table shows that women tend to earn lower wages than men. In the $20,000–$25,000 bracket and in each one below there are proportionately more women than men. The reverse is true in the higher brackets. That women's wages are low compared to men's can be explained by a concentration of women in low-paying jobs. Choice (1) is incorrect since income brackets have nothing to do with the number of workers. Neither choice (2) nor choice (4) explains the pattern of lower wages for women. Choice (3) is wrong since the table reports only full-time workers' wages.

25. **(4)** *Application/Behavioral Science.* Personality is part of the field of psychology. The other questions mentioned are most likely to interest researchers in other areas of social studies.

26. **(2)** *Analysis/Economics.* A solution to the trade deficit would have to include either spending less on imports or earning more from exports, or both. Limiting the quantity of imports would mean spending less on imports. Choice (5), which would have the opposite effect, can be eliminated. Choices (1), (3), and (4) are not related to the trade deficit problem.

27. **(2)** *Comprehension/Economics.* The cartoonist shows that the tax code book has grown in size and the tax professionals are smiling, meaning the tax reform has failed in its purpose to make taxes sim-

pler. Therefore choice (2) is correct. None of the other choices is supported by the cartoon.

28. **(4)** *Analysis/Geography.* Since a high standard of living requires energy, and coal and oil—on which we presently depend—exist in only limited supplies, we will have to depend more on other sources of energy. Increasing the human life span, in choice (1), would not increase our standard of living. Since a high standard of living depends on economic growth, slowing this growth, as in choice (2), would likely lower our standard of living. Since supplies of coal and oil are limited, choices (3) and (5) cannot be correct solutions.

29. **(1)** *Application/Economics.* In September, when the weather cools, the demand for air conditioners drops. When demand drops, prices usually drop. Therefore, buying an air conditioner in September would allow a consumer to take advantage of the demand/price relationship. In contrast, the consumer who buys a bathing suit in June—choice (5)—will likely find high prices. The situations in choices (2)–(4) are not related to the price/demand relationship.

30. **(4)** *Analysis/History.* All the laws mentioned ruled on whether slavery was to be allowed in new territories and states. The issues mentioned in the other choices are not discussed in these laws.

31. **(4)** *Comprehension/History.* The passage indicates that the debates and compromises were between senators from Northern states and senators from Southern states. Each side wanted to increase its strength by spreading its system to new territories.

32. **(3)** *Application/History.* Of the four laws mentioned, only the Compromise of 1850 and the Kansas–Nebraska Act state that the inhabitants of the territories would decide for themselves whether or not to adopt slavery.

33. **(5)** *Evaluation/History.* Congress continuously debated about and passed laws on the issue of slavery in the territories. But the laws it passed did not establish a consistent policy about allowing slavery or about leaving the decision on slavery to the people in the territories. Therefore, only choice (5) is supported.

34. **(3)** *Comprehension/Political Science.* The figure shows the many steps a bill can go through between its introduction and its passage. The statements in choices (1), (2), and (4) concern small details related to individual steps in the process. The statement in choice (5) is not shown in the chart.

35. **(3)** *Evaluation/Political Science.* Bills are considered and can be amended or killed at numerous points in the process, by various groups in both the House and the Senate. The system by which Congress handles bills is therefore one that involves careful consideration. The other choices are all contradicted—by specific points in the figure, in the case of choice (4); by the overall figure, in the case of choices (1), (2), and (5).

36. **(2)** *Comprehension/Political Science.* The figure shows that the floor of the House can send a bill back to a committee for further consideration. Therefore, the statement in choice (2) is incorrect.

37. **(2)** *Analysis/Political Science.* The figure shows two sets of double arrows connecting the conference committee with the House and Senate sides. The arrows are labeled "conflicts resolved." None of the other choices are supported by the figure.

38. **(1)** *Analysis/Political Science.* Porkbarrel legislation involves giving money to projects that aren't particularly useful but that will make voters happy. Satisfied voters may reelect the legislation's supporters. Choices (3) and (5) aren't likely, since the projects are described as useful. Choices (2) and (4) are also unlikely, especially since unnecessary projects waste government money.

39. **(3)** *Comprehension/History.* The rope that President Johnson is holding, labeled "Government programs," is far too short to reach the drowning figure labeled "Today's urban and poverty needs." Although the programs were, as one of the people on the pier says, "more than we've put out before," they weren't going to be enough to solve the country's urban and poverty problems.

40. **(5)** *Application/Geography.* The example discusses how a city, St. Petersburg, was founded and experienced rapid growth because it was on the Baltic Sea.

41. **(3)** *Application/Geography.* The example deals with the use of a natural resource and with how the environment influences both the need for and the availability of this resource.

42. **(2)** *Application/Geography.* The example shows how distribution of human population is limited by unfavorable environmental factors.

43. **(1)** *Application/Geography.* The example shows how early people's way of life changed because of environment factors.

44. **(4)** *Application/Geography.* The example discusses reasons for existing boundaries between nations in various parts of the world.

45. **(2)** *Analysis/Political Science.* The networks have been asked not to project presidential election winners to avoid affecting voter turnout on the West Coast. The only choice that suggests a possible change in voter turnout is (2). Early projections might make West Coast voters feel that the outcome had in effect already been determined so there was little point in their voting.

46. **(2)** *Application/History.* The United States was protesting against, and preparing to deal with, an act of interference by France, a European country, in the internal affairs of Mexico, a country in the Americas. Therefore, U.S. actions were based on the Monroe Doctrine.

47. **(2)** *Application/Economics.* Labor costs vary depending on how much a firm is producing: If the firm produces more, it generally must hire more labor and labor costs therefore increase; if the firm produces less, its labor needs and costs generally decrease. The costs mentioned in the other choices are all fixed costs, since they're not directly related to the firm's level of production.

48. **(5)** *Application/Behavioral Science.* Flying could bring out two phobias in a person: acrophobia (fear of heights) and claustrophobia (fear of closed places), so choice (5) is the best answer. Choice (1) is incorrect because if the restaurant is large and uncrowded, it probably has open space with few people; therefore, a panic attack would not be likely to occur in that situation. Choice (4) is also incorrect because few people would be taking a bus so early on a weekend morning. If someone has a pet, he/she would not fear it [choice (3)]. Smoking would calm one's nerves, not aggravate them.

49. **(2)** *Evaluation/History.* Jackson viewed government posts as "spoils of war" to which he, being the victor, was entitled. Jackson's appointments started what is now known as the "spoils system." The other choices, including the statement in choice (3) from Lincoln's Second Inaugural Address and that in choice (5) from John F. Kennedy's Inaugural Address, are essentially irrelevant to the situation described.

50. **(1)** *Comprehension/History.* Florida is east of the Louisiana Purchase but was acquired later. Choice (2) is true since the map shows some land was annexed, some purchased, and some acquired by treaty and that the United States obtained some land from both Britain and Mexico. The other choices can be established as true on the basis of information in the legend and/or the map itself.

51. **(1)** *Analysis/Political Science.* If members of Congress agree in advance that they'll vote for projects, these projects may not be questioned and examined as carefully as usual. There is nothing to support choices (2), (3), or (5). Choice (4) is, if anything, contradicted, since decisions to vote automatically for a bill should shorten, rather than lengthen, the process of passing the bill.

52. **(3)** *Analysis/Behavioral Science.* Choice (3), the incorrect statement, is the right answer. If IV (intravenous) drug abusers participated in needle-exchange programs, they would have traded in their "dirty" or infected needles for new, sterilized ones. Sharing needles, which involves the exchange of blood, is the way IV drug users contract AIDS. Choices (1) and (2) are correct statements because only by using latex or rubber condoms can a person protect him/herself against the HIV or AIDS virus during sexual intercourse.

53. **(5)** *Analysis/Behavioral Science.* Choice (5) is correct. Nurses and aides are more at risk of contracting AIDS because they have direct, day to day contact with AIDS patients for extended periods of time. All health care workers are supposed to be informed about and are required to take protective measures like wearing rubber gloves. Choice (2) is incorrect because surgeons, paramedics, and dentists also deal directly with blood.

54. **(3)** *Application/Political Science.* Choices (1) and (4) can be eliminated since the coattail effect applies only to candidates in the president's party. Choices (2) and (5) can also be eliminated, since to help other candidates from his party, the president must have voters' approval. Choice (3) is therefore right, especially since the coattail effect tends to benefit unknown candidates who lack a reputation of their own.

55. **(5)** *Comprehension/Economics.* Choices (1) and (2) relate to GNP, choice (3) to real GNP, and choice (4) to per capita GNP. Tax rates, in choice (5), however, have nothing to do with any of these.

56. **(3)** *Analysis/Economics.* Since China's GNP gets divided by so many more people than Sweden's, per capita GNP figures would show why China has a lower standard of living than Sweden even though its GNP is higher. None of the factors mentioned in the other choices could help explain the apparent contradiction.

57. **(1)** *Analysis/Economics.* Inflation artificially pushes the GNP up. Real GNP is what the GNP is once inflation has been taken into account. When inflation is high, the GNP will be artificially high but real GNP will not. Real GNP will be lower than the GNP. Choice (2) is incorrect, since if there is no inflation, GNP and real GNP should be equal. Choices (3)–(5) would not produce any difference between GNP and real GNP.

58. **(1)** *Application/Economics.* The president will want to point to the growth in the GNP, since this seems to show the economy is doing well. The challenger will want to focus on inflation and to point out that the growth in the GNP may largely reflect inflation. To do this, the challenger will focus on real GNP. Choice (2) must therefore be incorrect. Choice (3) is incorrect because nothing is said about the effects of population growth. Choices (4) and (5) are also not the best choices, since both the president and the challenger have an economic issue in their favor.

59. **(1)** *Evaluation/Behavioral Science.* Since the paragraph states that the trend is most evident in professional women over 30, it is logical to assume that they have careers. They had their first child after completing their education and working several years. There is nothing in the paragraph to support answers (2), (3), (4), and (5).

60. **(3)** *Comprehension/Political Science.* Since the House and the Senate are "checking" each other, bills essentially receive a double review. This more thorough process is also more lengthy, so choice (1) is contradicted. There is nothing to indicate that a bicameral system would have the effects described in choices (2), (4), and (5).

61. **(2)** *Comprehension/Behavioral Science.* The labels on the graph indicate that the higher the bar, the more nontraditional the attitudes about sex roles. The highest bar in the graph is for women in the unmarried couples life situation.

62. **(5)** *Evaluation/Behavioral Science.* In each of the four life situations, the bar for men is lower than the bar for women. Thus, the statement that men tend to have more traditional sex-role attitudes than women is supported by the figure. Choices (1) and (2) are not supported; if anything, the differences among people in the different life situations suggests that sex-role attitudes do not stay the same. Nothing is said about the effect of geographical area, as in choice (3), or of parents' attitudes, as in choice (4).

63. **(4)** *Evaluation/Geography.* The map shows that the Mountain and Pacific regions can produce 28 and 92.5 million kilowatts–far more than the amount possible anywhere else in the United States. Most of that power is potential because it has not yet been developed. Choice (1) is contradicted by the concentration of waterpower in the west. Contrary to choice (2), the Northeastern and New England states have developed less than half of their waterpower resources. Since the Midwestern states are shown as having developed some of their resources, choice (3) cannot be right. There is nothing in the map to support the sort of claim made in choice (5).

64. **(2)** *Comprehension/History.* France is shown as having a significant amount of North American territory in 1689, but none in 1763. It can therefore be concluded that between these two dates France was eliminated as a colonial power in North America. Choice (1) cannot be determined since South America is not shown. Choices (3), (4) and (5) all involve matters that cannot be determined from the two maps alone.

Simulated Test

1. **(3)** *Evaluation/Economics.* The budget deficit is related to the government's spending more money than it has taken in. Officials who want to eliminate deficits must therefore want the government's expenditures not to exceed its revenues. Choices (1), (4), and (5) are contradicted by the information. Choice (2) is not discussed.

2. **(3)** *Application/Economics.* Increasing the defense budget would add to the budget deficit. All the other choices would contribute to the goal of reducing the budget deficit, since the government would either be taking in more—choices (1), (2), and (5)—or spending less—choice (4).

3. **(3)** *Comprehension/History.* The man selling souvenirs and talking about selling junk shows how the historic significance of the occasion came second in the mind of some Americans. There is no support for the other choices.

4. **(4)** *Evaluation/History.* The cartoon says nothing about choices (2), (3), or (5) and contradicts choice (1).

5. **(2)** *Comprehension/History.* The map shows that the Hudson River runs into New York City. The Erie Canal, by linking Lake Erie and the Hudson River, gave New York a transportation link with areas west. None of the other canals or roads mentioned feed into New York.

6. **(3)** *Analysis/History.* All the roads and waterways shown link the East with what was then the West. Therefore, they would have increased trade in the east–west direction but would have done nothing to increase trade between the North and the South. All the other choices are logical consequences of the construction of these roads and waterways.

7. **(5)** *Application/Behavioral Science.* By breaking her difficult problem into smaller problems and trying to first solve these, the scientist is following a simplification strategy.

8. **(2)** *Application/Behavioral Science.* The staff is working backward, step by step, from a result that was undesirable to the starting point in the process that led to that result. It is therefore using the heuristic of working backward.

9. **(3)** *Application/Behavioral Science.* The company is trying out different ways of reaching its goal of improving supermarket sales. It learns from each attempt that fails and applies what it has learned to new attempts. The heuristic used is therefore trial and error.

10. **(4)** *Application/Behavioral Science.* The company wants to attract more customers and is trying out a solution that worked well for a competitor. In trying out a solution that is known to work, the company is using the analogous plans heuristic.

11. **(4)** *Comprehension/Economics.* The graph shows that increases in service and government jobs will more than make up for losses in manufacturing and agricultural jobs. There will therefore be an overall increase in the number of jobs. The graph does not have information to support the claims in choices (1) and (5). Choice (2) is contradicted, since the government sector will gain jobs. Choice (3) is also contradicted, since agriculture will lose more jobs than manufacturing.

12. **(5)** *Evaluation/Economics.* Since the $32,000 typically required to buy a new home is far more than many families earn, it's likely that some families will have to put off buying a home until they're in a better financial situation. Choice (1) is incorrect since $32,000 is just a typical figure and not an absolute requirement. Homes may now be more difficult to afford, but this doesn't mean that in the past everyone could buy a home, as in choice (2). Choice (3) is not supported by anything in the information. Choice (4) is too strong a conclusion to be drawn from the information given.

13. **(4)** *Comprehension/Political Science.* The horse and rider are ridiculously burdened with unnecessary "safety" equipment. Therefore, the cartoon's message is OSHA regulations are too numerous and in many cases not needed.

14. **(5)** *Analysis/History.* Since many of the working poor no longer have to pay taxes and tax rates are lower overall, the tax reform means lower taxes for many people. Choices (1) and (2) are therefore wrong. Choice (3) is not supported: The law reduced the number of different tax brackets from fifteen to two. Choice (4) is not supported: The law excused many working poor from paying taxes.

15. **(5)** *Analysis/Economics.* If the Consumer Price Index is up, goods and services cost more. Therefore consumers are getting less for their money. Choice (4), which makes the opposite claim, must be wrong. There is nothing in the information to support the claims in choices (1), (2), or (3).

16. **(3)** *Evaluation/Geography.* The Ganges River makes the plain through which it flows very fertile and capable of supporting many people. From this you can infer that the Ganges is important to India's economy. The passage indicates that the Himalayas, choice (2), have some of the world's highest mountains but not that they are directly important to India's

economy. There is nothing in the passage to support any of the other choices.

17. **(3)** *Evaluation/Political Science.* Railroads that went across country were an example of commerce crossing state boundaries and, as such, were to be regulated by Congress, not the states. Choices (1) and (5) are incorrect, since they just concern relations between states. Choice (2) is irrelevant since rate regulation is not a fine or bail. Choice (4) cannot explain the Supreme Court decision, since the decision said states could not regulate the railroads.

18. **(4)** *Comprehension/History.* Lincoln speaks of binding up the nation's wounds. This is in keeping with reuniting the nation after the war by bringing the South back into the Union. Choice (1) can be rejected: The image of binding up wounds does not relate to the idea of fighting. Nor does Lincoln want the South to be punished for its acts, as in choice (2), since he speaks of acting without malice and with charity. There is nothing in the quote to support the statements in choices (3) and (5).

19. **(3)** *Comprehension/Geography.* Choices (1) and (4) can both be eliminated, since Philadelphia and New York lost population between 1970 and 1980. Phoenix, choice (2), and Dallas–Ft. Worth, choice (5), had the largest gains of all cities, along with Houston and San Diego. Thus the correct response is choice (3).

20. **(2)** *Evaluation/Geography.* New York, Boston, Philadelphia, and other cities that lost population are located in the Northeast. Choices (1), (3), and (5) are contradicted by information in the map. There is nothing in the map to show a source of population gains, as in choice (4).

21. **(4)** *Comprehension/Behavioral Science.* The poverty rate for blacks was reduced from about 55 percent in 1959 to slightly over 30 percent in the remaining years shown. Choice (1) is true, since the drop in overall poverty rate between 1959 and 1969 was larger than that in any other period. Choice (2) is true: The figure for whites is always lower than the total figure. Choice (3) is true since there are increases from 1979 to 1985 in each column of the table. Choice (5) is supported since each figure in the total column is over 10 percent.

22. **(2)** *Analysis/Behavioral Science.* The passage states that ancient governments carried out censuses and that they used the information gained for such purposes as imposing taxes and raising an army. None of the other choices are implied in the passage.

23. **(2)** *Analysis/Geography.* Carbon dioxide, a pollutant released by the burning of fuels, is causing the atmosphere to keep more heat. This might eventually lead to a warming of the earth's climate. Nothing in the information suggests a relationship between the greenhouse effect and the problems mentioned in the other choices.

24. **(5)** *Application/Political Science.* Only choice (5) fits the description of a deviating election: The party out of power won, only to lose again in the next election.

25. **(1)** *Evaluation/Political Science.* The passage makes clear that election results are influenced both by long-term voting patterns, which are especially evident in maintaining elections and realigning elections, and immediate, election year issues and factors, which are especially evident in deviating elections. Choice (2) ignores the importance of long-term patterns and focuses on just one immediate issue. Choice (4) is contradicted by the discussion of deviating elections. Nothing is said in the passage to support choices (3) or (5).

26. **(1)** *Analysis/Political Science.* In maintaining elections voters keep electing the same party. People must be relatively happy with the way things are. It's unlikely that the country is going through great change and conflict, as in choice (2), or economic collapse, as in choice (3). There is no support for choices (4) or (5).

27. **(3)** *Comprehension/Economics.* The "wages adjusted for inflation" line compares buying power in each year to buying power in 1980. The lowest point in the graph between 1980 and 1984 (the five years that make up the choice in this item) is 1982.

28. **(4)** *Analysis/Economics.* Wages rose by $74 between 1980 and 1987; therefore, choices (3) and (5) are wrong. However, workers' weekly wages would not buy as much in 1987 as in 1980. In 1980, a week's pay bought $235 worth of goods. In 1987, a week's pay would purchase only $227 worth of goods by 1980 standards. Therefore, prices went up more than wages. Since wages did not keep up with inflation, choice (2) is wrong. There is nothing about choice (1) in the graphs.

29. **(2)** *Analysis/Geography.* A move from a rural area to a city fits the definition of hierarchical migration, since cities are larger than rural towns and villages. Moreover, the existence of opportunities in cities is a strong motive for migrating. Choices (1) and (5) can be eliminated, since hierarchical migration deals with movement within a country, not between countries. Problems in cities, in choice (3), would not provide a reason for migrating to cities. Improved transportation systems, in choice (4), cannot explain why migration is more likely to be from smaller to larger places.

30. **(2)** *Application/Political Science.* The Constitution does not specifically say that Congress can establish a national bank. But such a bank is necessary if Congress is to carry out other powers that the Constitution does specifically give it. Therefore, this example involves an implied power.

31. **(5)** *Application/Political Science.* The federal and state governments are separately exercising the same power to tax citizens. All the other choices can be ruled out, since both federal and state governments exercise the power to tax citizens.

32. **(3)** *Application/Political Science.* The example describes powers that the Constitution specifically denies to governments. All the other choices are wrong.

33. **(1)** *Application/Political Science.* The example illustrates specific, enumerated powers. Choice (2) is wrong because the powers are clearly specified in the Constitution. Choice (3) is directly contradicted by the example. Choices (4) and (5) are wrong since the powers mentioned are given to Congress, that is, to the federal government.

34. **(2)** *Application/Economics.* Lower prices lead producers to produce less; higher prices lead them to produce more. Thus choice (2) is correct and choice (1) must be wrong. Choice (4) does not make sense, and choice (3) is wrong because increased prices depend on increased demand. Choice (5) is unlikely, since the relatively low price of corn indicates demand must be down; farmers, if anything, would want to increase demand.

35. **(4)** *Evaluation/Economics.* The two people on the treadmill of wages and prices are trying to keep up with the cost of living. No matter how fast they move, they are still in the same place. This doesn't indicate that they can't meet their basic needs, as in choice (3), or that their incomes are falling way behind the cost of living, as in choice (5). The title suggests choice (2), but the "person" that figures are trying to keep up with is really an economic condition, not an individual. Nor is the "person" big business, as in choice (1).

36. **(3)** *Comprehension/Behavioral Science.* Pasteur is saying that sudden insight into a problem is in fact not entirely accidental. Insights "come" to people whose minds are prepared—that is, people who have thought a lot about the problem.

37. **(1)** *Analysis/Political Science.* Choices (2) and (5) can be ruled out, since the Hatch Act prohibits government workers from engaging in certain political activities. This prohibition is better explained by choice (1): Government workers, by virtue of their positions, could have too much influence on elections, and the Hatch Act is a means of preventing this. Choices (3) and (4) are not supported by anything in the information.

38. **(1)** *Comprehension/History.* The passage discusses what President Eisenhower meant by the military-industrial complex and his fear that it might gain too much influence over government decision making. Choice (4) is contradicted by the passage. Choices (2), (3), and (5) are not discussed.

39. **(4)** *Analysis/History.* Although military industries usually shrank after wars, cold war tensions made it desirable for U.S. industry to keep producing weapons. President Eisenhower discussed the military-industrial complex, but he did not advise that it be created, as in choice (3). Choices (1), (2), and (5) are not mentioned in the passage.

40. **(4)** *Evaluation/History.* According to the passage, President Eisenhower viewed the military-industrial complex as necessary, because of cold war tensions, but also as dangerous.

41. **(3)** *Application/History.* President Eisenhower said that one danger of the military-industrial complex was that it could lead to unnecessary spending. Therefore, Eisenhower presumably would approve that Congress closely examine military budgets. Choices (1) and (2) can be ruled out, since Eisenhower felt activities of the military-industrial complex were for the most part necessary. Choices (4) and (5) can also be ruled out, since these are the sorts of dangers Eisenhower was warning against.

42. **(4)** *Evaluation/History.* Besides the Bill of Rights only five amendments were added in the eighteenth and nineteenth centuries. The remaining eleven amendments were all added in the twentieth century. Choice (1) cannot be supported since the amendments have been passed at certain times but not others. Choices (2) and (3) cannot be supported, especially since there have been relatively few amendments. The time line shows nothing about the content of the amendments, as in choice (5).

43. **(4)** *Analysis/Behavioral Science.* The passage mentions that research supports the view that mental states affect physical ones and that this particular research found a relationship between loneliness and low levels of cells that combat viruses. Thus choice (4) correctly states the hypothesis. Choice (1) reverses the direction of cause and effect; the research was investigating effects of mental states on physical ones. Nothing is said about comparing the effects of different mental states, so choice (2) can be ruled out. The statement in choice (3) is a background assumption of the study. The research did not show or investigate whether being happy diminishes the likelihood of getting sick, as in choice (5).

44. **(1)** *Evaluation/Political Science.* The chart shows U.S. public opinion influences presidential decisions about foreign policy. Choice (2) is incorrect since the chart shows the staff as simply providing input for decisions. The chart does not address the topics in choices (3) and (4). Choice (5) is not supported: The chart does not indicate whether any executive agencies are more important than others.

45. **(4)** *Application/Political Science.* The fact that the Senate must confirm treaties the president makes means that the president cannot act without the approval of the legislative branch. The statement in choice (1) does not involve a check. Choices (2) and (3) can be eliminated since they involve foreign countries and an international organization rather than a branch of the U.S. government. Choice (5) can also be eliminated, since the agencies all belong to the executive branch.

46. **(3)** *Analysis/History.* The graph shows that the North had considerable advantages over the South in number of states, population, industry, and financial resources. Therefore choice (1) is wrong. Choice (2) can be ruled out, since the graph shows the North as being in a better position. The graph shows nothing about terrain, in choice (4). Although the graph shows the North as having considerable advantages, it does not establish that the South could not have won the war.

47. **(4)** *Analysis/Political Science.* If Congress attaches a measure that it wants passed to a bill the president considers important, Congress has a good chance of getting the measure passed. The president won't want to veto a bill he cares about, so Congress's rider becomes law, along with the bill. Choice (2) is wrong since the president can't edit bills. Choice (3) is wrong, since riders are measures Congress wants passed. Choices (1) and (5) are not supported by the information.

48. **(3)** *Analysis/Geography.* The information indicates that until fairly recently the United States was almost self-sufficient in minerals and also that Americans are major consumers of minerals. It is therefore likely that shortages are the result of heavy consumption. None of the other choices are suggested by the information; choices (1) and (4) are, if anything, contradicted.

49. **(3)** *Evaluation/Geography.* If there were more people, it would be hard to reduce total consumption. Each of the other four choices would aid conservation of mineral resources.

50. **(3)** *Comprehension/Geography.* Minerals occur unevenly in the earth's crust, so only large size increases a country's chances of having varied mineral resources. The information does not suggest that either hemisphere or particular types of land forms yield greater mineral resources—choices (1), (4), and (5). Choice (2) is not logical since large consumers may import the resources they consume.

51. **(3)** *Analysis/Geography.* Some minerals can no longer be found in high-grade deposits. They are still obtainable, but with greater cost and efforts. Choices (1), (4), and (5) are all contradicted by the information. Technology has developed mineral substitutes but has not increased resources, as in choice (2).

52. **(1)** *Comprehension/Behavioral Science.* In 1900, 22 percent of the population was in the 0 –14 age group. This percentage was the smallest for that group.

53. **(5)** *Comprehension/Behavioral Science.* In 1940, the 35-54 age group contained 26 percent of the population, a greater percentage than in any of the other years

shown. Choices (1)–(4) are contradicted by information in the graph.

54. **(2)** *Analysis/Behavioral Science.* The two youngest age groups made up a smaller portion of the population in 1980 than in 1900; the two oldest age groups, a larger portion. Therefore, the population in 1980 was older than in 1900. The graph contradicts choice (3). The graph has no information about wealth—choice (1)—or population size—choices (4) and (5).

55. **(1)** *Application/Behavioral Science.* The main trend in the graph is the aging of America's population. Since older people are likely to require more medical care, expansion in healthcare facilities will probably be needed. Choices (2)–(4) are wrong: Because the birthrate must be going down, there should be less need for new jobs, housing, and schools. The graph has no data that would indicate the need for new prisons—choice (5).

56. **(2)** *Application/Economics.* Concern with the growth of the money supply distinguishes monetarism, as does the rejection of other forms of government action, such as spending.

57. **(4)** *Application/Economics.* Keynesians believe that the government should stimulate the economy in times when it cannot correct itself. A depression is such a time, and a public works program helps to stimulate the economy.

58. **(3)** *Application/Economics.* The supply-side approach believes lower taxes give businesses extra income to invest and more incentive to do so.

59. **(1)** *Application/Economics.* The idea underlying the laissez-faire approach is clearly expressed here: The economy works best if left alone; the government should not attempt to correct it.

60. **(3)** *Evaluation/History.* As a clergyman, King objected to the Vietnam War on moral grounds. U.S. bombing destroyed entire villages of women and children in the countryside and forests and farmland that provided the population with food. Furthermore, he thought the U.S. was morally wrong to support Thieu, "a brutal dictator."

61. **(5)** *Application/History.* If King were living today, he most probably would have supported the Chinese students protesting for more freedom, the release of Nelson Mandela fighting for equal rights for African people in South Africa, and the return to power of the Haitian President Aristide who was democratically elected; therefore, choices (1)–(3) are not the correct answers because they involve the suppression or denial of freedom. Accordingly, choice (4) is also incorrect. The best choice is (5) because the Soviet Republics fought to demand their freedom or autonomy from the Soviet government.

62. **(3)** *Analysis/Geography.* According to the graph, the single, largest beach polluter is plastic, 64%. Choice (3) is, therefore, correct because balloons and plastic bags fall under the 64%. All other choices deal with less significant sources of beach and ocean pollution: metal, 10.2%; glass, 10.1%; paper, 9.9%; and rubber (tires), 2%.

63. **(1)** *Analysis/History.* Choices (2)–(5) are facts that can be proven. Choice (1) is the opinion of the "pro-life" activists who are fighting to outlaw abortion. "Murder" is an emotionally-charged word, and the assertion that "abortion is murder" is debated by the "pro-choice" activists who favor a woman's right to have a legal abortion if that is her choice.

64. **(4)** *Analysis/History.* Since the abortion issue is being debated, both sides are actively fighting for their position, so choices (1) and (2) are logical results. With the Supreme Court's ruling of Webster v. Reproductive Health Services, a woman's right to have a legal abortion has been limited by the states; therefore, you would expect the number of legal abortions performed in the U.S. to be reduced. Thus, choice (4) is the correct answer. Because the debate has been "stormy," it is logical to assume abortion was a major issue in the 1992 Presidential election.